RAISED IN A Bottle

Free yourself from
a childhood
with alcoholism.

KRISTINA HERMANN

Copyright KRISTINA HERMANN 2020c
Published by BUOY MEDIA LLC
All rights reserved.

No part of this book may be reproduced, scanned, or distributed in any printed or electronic form without permission from the author.
The Author holds exclusive rights to this work. Unauthorized duplication is prohibited.

Cover design by Juan Villar Padron,
https://www.juanjpadron.com

Special thanks to my editor Janell Parque
http://janellparque.blogspot.com/

Connect with Kristina online:

Author website:
https://kristina-hermann.dk/en/home/

Facebook:
https://www.facebook.com/raisedinabottlekristinahermann

Instagram:
https://www.instagram.com/kristinahermannpsychotherapist/

Twitter:
https://twitter.com/HermannPsy

LinkedIn:
https://www.linkedin.com/in/kristina-hermann-8492031b2/

Vimeo:
https://vimeo.com/user37844714

The book is dedicated to my siblings: Elizabeth, Jakob, Henriette, Robin, and Bo.

Contents

- PROLOGUE 5
- INTRODUCTION 11
- HOW TO USE THIS WORKBOOK 16
- FACING THE REALITY OF FAMILIES SHAPED BY ALCOHOL PROBLEMS 20
- LEARNING TO "HOLD MIND IN MIND" 28
- TELLING YOUR OWN STORY 39
- DIFFICULT FEELINGS 46
  - *EXERCISE: WRITE YOUR LIFE STORY* *62*
- EMOTIONAL TRIGGERS 66
  - *EXERCISE: WRITE YOUR LIFE STORY* *72*
- SELF-ESTEEM 73
  - *EXERCISE: WRITE YOUR LIFE STORY* *89*
- LETTING GO OF TRAUMA AND GROUNDING YOURSELF IN YOUR BODY 90
  - *EXERCISE: WRITE YOUR LIFE STORY* *106*
- NEEDS - MET AND UNMET 107
  - *EXERCISE: WRITE YOUR LIFE STORY* *115*
- BE YOUR OWN LOVING PARENT, BECOME YOUR OWN BEST FRIEND 116
  - *EXERCISE: WRITE YOUR LIFE STORY* *122*
- RECOGNIZE THE ROLES YOU PLAY 123
  - *EXERCISE: WRITE YOUR LIFE STORY* *139*
- PUTTING THE BRAKES ON UNHEALTHY INVOLVEMENT 140
  - *EXERCISE: WRITE YOUR LIFE STORY* *150*
- SAY GOODBYE TO DRAMA IN RELATIONSHIPS 151
  - *EXERCISE: WRITE YOUR LIFE STORY* *158*
- YOU HAVE THE RIGHT… 160
  - *EXERCISE: WRITE YOUR LIFE STORY* *163*
- CHOOSE YOUR VALUES 165
- BELIEVE IN THE FUTURE 170
- FINAL THOUGHTS 177
- ACKNOWLEDGMENTS 181
- NOTES 182
- BIBLIOGRAPHY 192
- ABOUT THE AUTHOR 201

Prologue

Why I Wrote This Book

Raised in a Bottle is intended as a steady, loving hand in support of anyone seeking to work through and overcome the challenges of having grown up with a parent who had an alcohol abuse problem. When a parent drinks, everyone in the family is affected, and children, in particular, have no way out. Addiction problems in the home not only can deprive a child of a childhood, but they also plant the seeds of an adulthood that can lack clear, stable boundaries and the inner foundation of care and support needed for a full, rich life.

In a family burdened by substance abuse, relationships are organized around the addiction rather than meeting the children's developmental needs. The energy that would normally be channeled into building a child's complete personality gets redirected to devising survival strategies, such as assuming a caregiving role for parents and siblings.

It has long been understood that children raised in such environments are forced to become adults prematurely; in fact, the term "adult child" was coined to describe them. This rush to adulthood bypasses some of the child's most essential formative experiences. She never gets the chance to be a child, receiving no support in playing and exploring, facing challenges, responding to curiosity, or enjoying childhood freedoms. Vital guidance, care, training, and protection are simply missing, and she doesn't learn how to take care of herself, whether physically, socially, or emotionally.

Someone with these gaps in her upbringing may have difficulty seeing herself clearly, accurately perceiving how and where she fits into the larger world. She may misidentify negative elements of her younger years, taking them for parts of her own personality worthy of shame or blame, when in actuality, they are products of her parent's addiction. As an adult, she may not realize that personal difficulties such as relationship problems, low self-esteem, erratic moods, unhealthy coping strategies, and feelings of abandonment or alienation and loneliness did not originate within her. Instead, they are the toxic legacy of alcohol abuse.

A Book That Is Long Overdue

Decades have passed since researchers began their focused inquiry into the consequences of alcohol and substance abuse. And as scientific understanding of addiction has advanced, so has insight into the myriad negative consequences of childhood exposure to alcohol abuse in the home, consequences that can manifest strongly in adulthood.

And yet, while there are growing numbers of treatment options for people with addictions, far fewer exist for those affected by substance abuse on the part of another family member. As a society, we remain alarmingly backward when it comes to repairing the damage done to children in such families—neither the children nor the adults they become are getting the treatment and interventions they need. Consequently, they can still end up facing a wide range of relationship problems and other psychological damage alone.

Most of the available and commonly recommended self-help books for "adult children" date from the 1980s and don't benefit from recent research. They generally draw on AA's Twelve Steps —a program dating back to the 1930s, when treatment for people with alcohol problems was almost nonexistent, and a system based on religious belief was the most practical and perhaps the only avenue for addressing this clear need.

Now, nearly a half-century old, ACA (Adult Children of Alcoholics) emerged in the wake of AA, along with a number of other adherents of the 12-step method, to provide help for young people and adults with group meetings, literature, and 12-step work. The problem is that ACA transfers the fundamental approach for alcoholics to their adult children. That shift is not necessarily helpful for individuals whose youthful development was affected by a substance-abusing parent. It may even do serious harm since it leaves the individual with a high risk of retaining dysfunctional identification—of seeing himself as deeply flawed. A more elaborate, evidence-based, empowering self-help program is needed to provide adult children with the tools to reclaim their own lives.

While the literature and concepts that AA's founder, Bill Wilson, formulated may have remained unchanged over the last 30 to 50 years, rapid development has taken place in the field of psychology. For example, neuroaffective developmental psychology, which follows the brain's emotional development from the fetal state onward, is revealing how emotions constitute the entire link between people and are central to attachment.

Based on this new knowledge, new psychotherapeutic treatment methods are emerging that may indicate viable, (re)constructive paths to take in supporting the developmental process of attachment, personality development, emotional expression, and social skills (e.g., mentalization-based psychotherapy for families and people with poor mental capacity) and insecure attachment patterns. As Daniel Stern emphasizes in relation to the child's developmental potential, "We are all born to participate in each other's nervous system." Because exposure to substance abuse severely jeopardizes a child's development, any sound course of treatment must include the retroactive repair of developmental shortcomings carried into adulthood.

This workbook aims to bridge the enormous shortfall in treatment for adult children and catch up with current knowledge and methods to provide meaningful, substantive help. Based on a wide range of methodologies and newer techniques for fostering personal development, it draws a direct connection between a young person's natural responses to the dysfunction in an alcoholic household and the inner struggles that may develop later in life. It guides the reader through exercises aimed at mending the flaws and further exploring traits and skills he may never have had the opportunity to develop properly. Chapter by chapter, the reader will come to understand himself better, ultimately freeing himself from debilitating patterns of behavior.

Note that this book can be an especially effective resource used in tandem with talk therapy, either individual or group, where it can serve as a powerful resource for therapists.

A Broad-Based, Integrative Approach

The primary content and sequencing of the chapters are guided by evidence-based methods with proven outcomes. As it happens, few of them were developed specifically for people raised in homes marked by substance abuse, but through my many years of work as a therapist, I have found these approaches, exercises, and tools to be extremely effective.

The primary theorists I draw upon are Peter Steinglass, John Bowlby, Daniel Stern, Anthony Bateman, and Peter Fonagy, as well as Peter Levine. Additionally, I have found Claudia Black's description of children's roles—the hero child, the scapegoat child, the forgotten child, the clown child—useful in helping people recognize and break out of old patterns. Transactional psychologist Stephen Karpman's drama triangle is another important tool for tackling one's problems with attachment, identity formation, emotional understanding, and trauma. For building self-esteem, Louise Hay's affirmations are a valuable resource. These models provide important symbolic structures to cognitively anchor and support the inner work of the reader.

The psychiatrists and psychoanalysts Daniel Stern and John Bowlby have individually researched how we establish basic patterns in our psyche in childhood. Both have thoroughly investigated the importance of how, for example, a toddler is greeted by her parents and the consequences this interaction has for her self-esteem and identity formation. Bowlby's attachment theory describes four attachment patterns: one safe and three others that are insecure. There is a high risk that children from families with abuse will grow up with an insecure attachment pattern, as parental functioning is significantly impaired by alcohol abuse.

Anthony Bateman and Peter Fonagy's mentalization-based approach—"holding mind in mind"—offers a powerful aid toward developing an understanding of both self and others, learning to hold both in one's consciousness. Peter Levine's concept of trauma rooted in perceived threat or overwhelming experience plays another key role in the book. The array of hazards to members of addiction-affected families leaves them vulnerable to significant trauma. Left unaddressed, that trauma can throttle emotional energy and greatly limit the experience of happiness, vitality, and courage in life.

My Hopes for You

Raised in a Bottle embodies my heartfelt belief that, despite a tough upbringing in a family that knew substance abuse, you can flourish and find your way to a life of joy, abundance, and love. It seeks to assure you that it is not up to a distant, unhappy past to dictate what your life will be like *now*, to mandate what you will succeed or fail at, what will give you pleasure, and what will cause you pain.

I intend for this book and its interwoven web of methodologies to hold the reader's hand and offer a comforting—but forceful and confident—reminder that he or she is not alone. Its program is designed to help you shift the focus of energy in your life from times and places long past to the *here and now* and provide you with the dignity, clarity, independence, and personal power you need to find fulfillment. I sincerely wish you the best of luck in your efforts.

Introduction

"The way he opened the door after a stressful day was the first clue, and I could tell from the sound of his footsteps when something was wrong again. First, he'd open the cupboard and take out two glasses—a tumbler and a shot glass. One was for beer; the other was for liquor. Those two drinks would quickly turn to several, and his mood would change; he'd become either more relaxed or more angry. In that unsettling atmosphere, the world could turn upside down at any moment."—Mona

Chances are if you are the child of someone with an addiction to alcohol, your upbringing likely left you unprepared for life as an adult. Regardless of a family's economic or educational level, alcohol abuse disrupts and distorts its fundamental structure and the health of its members. The consequences of that distortion are clear, common, and long-lasting.

You could compare it to living in a poorly built house, one whose foundation was not fully poured and didn't have a chance to set before the walls went up. A house like that does not provide the security that other houses do. With the cracks in its foundation, its wobbly walls, and its ill-fitting doors, it offers neither shelter nor safety from intruders.

A family that goes from crisis to crisis, one painful event to another, managing merely to survive, never develops a healthy, genuinely positive narrative about itself. Its sense of its own history and identity gets distorted into something negative, which can leave a child without an anchor for his or her own personal identity.

Growing up in a family with alcohol problems forced you into roles that compromised your identity and prevented you from growing into your own authentic self. Rather than being nurtured in discovering and developing your own unique abilities, perhaps you had to take on responsibilities that belong to parents in healthy families. Maybe you adopted your parents' unhealthy and ineffective problem-solving patterns, leaving you inclined to try to avoid life's challenges rather than stepping up to face them with competence and confidence.

If your parents were unable to meet your needs as a child, they might have left you with pain that lingers to this day. For a child, lying awake at night with no one to come and comfort you in your sadness or fear, or being repeatedly left alone and at the mercy of chance, eventually translates into insecurity, low self-esteem, and little ability to feel joy and to trust. The trauma of childhood neglect can have long-lasting physical implications for the adult body and impair your ability to care for yourself, and even leave you prone to addiction as a way to try and self-soothe.

Along with neglect, the blurring of boundaries in childhood can turn certain feelings, both yours and other peoples', into foreign territory. You may end up afraid of other people's feelings or unable to trust the possibility that someone else might be interested in yours. Because the very notion of limits and boundaries has never been clear, you find it difficult to sense your position in a social context or even in a room. Where you stand in terms of the difference between right and wrong, between your own values and those of others, and between appropriate and inappropriate behavior may be hard for you to grasp.

Often, a person with a family background of alcohol abuse has learned to be a kind of seismograph, quietly recording everything happening around him and vigilantly monitoring the emotional environment. Perhaps your fear of making a negative impression on people, whether on the job or in social settings, influences everything you do; rather than being conscious of your own value, you adapt yourself to fit in wherever you go and continuously seek affirmation from other people. A completely harmless invitation to a meeting with a boss might trigger panic reactions as you fantasize over expectations of reprimands or even firing —even if you know that you do your work well and work harder than many of your colleagues.

By contrast, an upbringing that lacked healthy boundaries may have left you unusually tolerant, understanding, and accommodating of other people and their peculiarities, to the point that you find it too easy to invite people with addictions into your life since their problems don't strike you as abnormal. Such relationships generally end up fraught with painful drama—the closer the personal connection becomes, the more volatile the situation can be.

Perhaps you have experienced yourself overreacting when your partner was late for an appointment or resented the way your teenage son's sullen reply to an innocent question threw you off balance or taken a friend's harmless opinion as a direct criticism of you. For a person without the peace of mind to weather situations like these and the faith that she will come out of them unscathed, real, close connections with others can seem to get endlessly sabotaged. At the same time, the path to your goals in life is always susceptible to being derailed.

An Unfinished House

Once again, picture your personality as a house. The foundation of that house is your self-esteem, how you perceive your own value. Whether it's high or low, your self-esteem is at the root of how you live your life, and if that foundation is shaky, its instability will affect everything you do. Continually struggling to shore up an unsteady house is hard work, and the extra effort can end up costing you: Precious elements of your personality may develop in only a limited way or simply never get the chance to surface in the first place.

A house is meant to shelter and protect, provide you with the time, space, and security to learn who you are and be that. Its walls and doors are intended to be reliable and secure, boundaries that let you include what you want and need in your life and exclude what you don't. There is no question that those are your decisions to make, but unless you're on a firm footing, steady on your foundation, you may not have the confidence to make them. You may find that there's room in your house for everyone's problems but your own.

It may feel to you as if, no matter how much you work on it, your own house doesn't seem to welcome you; its atmosphere is dark and sad rather than bright and warm. Instead of cheering you up, encouraging you to thrive, it leaves you blaming yourself, berating yourself for the house's imperfections and incompleteness. You may even get the feeling that everyone has an ideal house, but you and that yours will never be worth having until it is identical to theirs.

Things shouldn't be that way: Your home shouldn't feel vulnerable to you or inhospitable or inferior. Real repairs may be needed to put your house on a firm foundation, and this book offers you the tools to make those repairs. Will they be easy? Probably not; there may even be some inner part of you that fears the uncertainty that can come with change, even change for the better.

Your focus right now may be on simply getting through one day at a time, putting out a thousand little fires that threaten to burn down your house—but shifting that focus, making the necessary repairs can bring great rewards. Relieved of the constant demands and distractions of one crisis after another, you can begin to expect more out of life, and demand more, and *get* more. With your foundation made secure and reliable, you can dare to believe in a happy, productive future. And *believing it will bring it*.

How to use this workbook

This book is intended to support you in learning new, healthier ways of being with yourself and interacting with others. It is designed to guide you, step by step, through the repairs and adjustments that will get your life on track. Each of its exercises aims to bring you into closer touch with yourself, to help you let go of survival mechanisms and reactive behaviors that have worked against you, and to help you develop the ability to both set boundaries and build the sorts of bridges that make for healthy intimacy with other people.

The exercises will affect you in various ways. Some will trigger *Aha!* moments, as you become aware of unhealthy survival mechanisms that you developed for dealing with your family. Others may open your eyes to a spacious place inside you where you and your feelings can coexist rather than always being at odds with each other, a place where it is easier for you to accept and appreciate your whole self. Still others will help equip you with the outlook and tools for coping with intense emotions such as anger or deep sadness. In combination, the exercises will help you do the physical, mental, and emotional work of getting in touch with who you really are.

If you find that certain sections or chapters seem especially relevant to you, don't be afraid to give them extra attention. Spend more time on them and look up the books referenced there for further information. If you're able to pinpoint an issue that's especially relevant to you, you may want to begin a course of therapy to address it. There is no more important use of your time than this; be sure to give it as much time as it needs.

You can boost the therapeutic value of many of the exercises by doing them with others with whom you feel safe and secure. If you are currently in therapy, involve your practitioner or therapist in the exercises. If you are part of a group whose participants know each other well, try doing the exercises together, or do them separately at home and then discuss them as a group.

What Changes Do You Want to Make?

As you embark on the work in this book, take a moment to consider where you'd like to see the most significant change in your life and which topics may be most meaningful for you. Which of the potential changes listed below might have the most dramatic and positive impact on you? Select a handful of them as specific places for your developmental work to begin.

I want to learn how to set limits in a clear and equitable manner without feeling guilty afterward.

I want to be calm rather than troubled and burdened by rumination and worry.

I want to understand that my parents' problems are basically not my responsibility, and I want to release myself from my old pattern of taking over when they have difficulties.

I want to stop isolating myself and falling into "black holes," where I find it difficult to talk to others.

I want to take good care of myself.

I want to have clarity in relating to my mother, father, and siblings.

I want to understand myself, my feelings, and my reactions.

I want to be able to return myself to a state of calm when my emotions get too intense.

I want to let go of the view that I am different from others, so I can be comfortable in communities.

I want to get rid of my inner critic.

I want to lose my excessive need to assume responsibility for how others feel.

I want to get to know myself so that I can shape my life in relation to my own needs and dreams.

I want to break the pattern in which I was raised by giving my kids attention, being present for them, and encouraging their independence.

I want to learn to be in close relationships, so I know what it is that creates security.

I want to be able to send clear signals about what I want, rather than hiding my needs.

I want to know how to build up my self-esteem.

I want to love myself and take responsibility for my life and my choices.

I want to be capable of discerning whether other people are keeping me trapped in my old patterns, or instead, providing the sustenance and support to let me be me.

I want my moods to be more stable and no longer experience sudden mood swings.

I want to become more knowledgeable about problems caused by alcohol abuse and how it has influenced me and my family.

All self-improvement begins with becoming conscious of your patterns. As long as a pattern such as a defensive mechanism remains unconscious, your reactions will be automatic, and you won't fully understand the pattern's cause or function. You won't see the reality of the situation as it truly is, and you will likewise be unaware of how damaging your reactions can be to yourself and the people close to you. This book will guide you through those specific areas of life that are commonly shaped and affected by an upbringing in a home marked by alcohol abuse.

In working with this book, you will come to discover, again and again, sides of yourself you were not aware of, as well as previously hidden causes behind the way you act and feel in particular situations. That new knowledge will let you say goodbye to patterns or stories about yourself that are no longer useful or constructive. It will become clear that, while certain ways of dealing with the world may have helped you maintain control when you were young, as an adult, they only pull the rug out from under you and generate disappointment, misunderstanding, and frustration.

1

FACING THE REALITY OF FAMILIES SHAPED BY ALCOHOL PROBLEMS

"Our home was dominated by alcohol, and my mother was very unstable. I remember once she forgot to pick me up from kindergarten, and I sat with a teacher, staring out the window, waiting for her. There was talk about whether to call someone from child protective services because they couldn't get ahold of her. I didn't understand how she didn't see my pain and the fact that I was even alive. There wasn't always money, and we ate mostly junk food. My clothes were often dirty, and I hadn't necessarily had a bath. Maybe I was just good at hiding it all, being the quiet, good little girl." —Lene

In a household where alcohol is being abused, the rules are different. Many people realize only later in life that a parent was actually addicted, that there was a reason their father was so unfriendly, and people never came to visit. As children, they witnessed behavior that didn't seem quite right, but without grasping the reasons behind it. Time after time, they found themselves in situations they didn't understand, but the feelings aroused by those situations were never put into words.

A child growing up in that kind of environment learns to live with uncertainty. She can't trust her own senses; she never fully understands what is going on at home, and when she makes her way into other people's homes, she doesn't understand what goes on there, either. She lacks an internal compass—the one her parents never instilled in her—and that makes navigating both her immediate surroundings and the world at large a challenge.

When you cannot trust your own perceptions, relating to other people can be confusing. A child accustomed to being in precarious situations with a drunk parent—his mother driving intoxicated with him in the passenger seat, his father talking drunken nonsense—may develop an exaggerated tolerance for such behavior and come to see it as normal. Being unable to distinguish strange, unhealthy conduct from normal conduct leaves him less able to protect and take care of himself.

Accustomed to a high level of internal stress and also used to being treated harshly, a child of someone with an addiction often doesn't know what sort of treatment to expect from people outside his home. His perceptions of whether a particular friendship may be good for him or bad can't be relied upon. And that handicap can persist long after childhood, making him unusually vulnerable to risks and risky environments.

All families have a powerful drive toward togetherness, but interactions and conversations in a family with alcohol problems can be irrational and difficult to understand. No one dares confront the parents for fear the family will start to break apart. Furthermore, these families often harbor a hostile attitude toward other people, an "us vs. them" mentality—"We are right, and they are wrong." This is a common trait among families with significant problems, and it brings with it a resistance to seeking help because they believe that other people should not interfere in their lives. Does that sound familiar to you? Has it ever prevented you from seeking help?

"I lay on my bed, panic-stricken, with my heart racing and the anxiety rattling my whole body. He burst through the door with rage in his eyes and slammed his hand down on my desk, sending my neatly arranged cassettes flying around the room. All my efforts to keep my room clean and clear were undone by the chaos. He shouted in anger, slammed the door, and left me lying there. The pain wouldn't stop, and my mother never came in. What I had done wrong and what I was being punished for, I never understood."—Mona

Honesty can be in short supply among people with addictions. Sometimes a person actually believes that since he is able to maintain his job and has never gone berserk or become destructive at home, his excessive drinking must go unnoticed by the rest of the family. Even someone who is in recovery might confidently assure his grown child that he or she was brought up "just fine," and the drinking didn't have any impact. But while there may have been ways in which the home functioned fairly well, alcoholism *always* affects the children, and never for the better.

Addiction makes it hard for a person to see herself objectively, and, in fact, as dependency progresses, it harms the part of the brain that deals with self-reflection. Not surprisingly, that carries over into her comprehension of other people as well. With an addiction playing out, the ability to read others' signals and empathize with them degrades along with self-awareness, while self-absorption increases.

Raised in a Bottle

Picture a drunk father with no understanding of how his addiction has affected him—is he any more likely to understand its impact on his son? On the other hand, the child seems to have a clear view of his father's condition—namely, drunk and sloppy—but there's a good chance he'll receive no validation from anyone that what he is seeing is what it appears to be. In fact, the whole household seems to conspire to camouflage what is really happening. Once this has gone on long enough, the biggest question in the boy's mind becomes, "What is really happening?"

If you grew up with a parent with an addiction, many of the conversations you had were with someone who was intoxicated, and those conversations did not make sense—they went around in circles or veered wildly off-topic. Your efforts to communicate may have been met with rejection or shaming or dismissal. Over time, the failure to get real answers to your questions may have ground down your natural curiosity, bit by bit, and you simply got used to not listening to people anymore. Unable to count on what your parents told you, you were forced to rely on your own assumptions of what the world was about.

And what guarantee did you have that those assumptions were correct?

"Of all our family, my mother was the upset, angry one. She'd get so angry she might not talk to me for several days. No matter how much I cried and apologized, she wouldn't give in. It was so terrible. I was so sad, so sad it made my stomach ache. I didn't realize at that time that what was making our family life so hard was her drinking."—Charlotte

A parent with an addiction frequently uses words as a kind of weapon to cover up something or manipulate a child. She might say things she doesn't mean or can't deliver on. The aim is sometimes to distract the child from things that have gone wrong in the home. This can take the form of lavish promises: "We're going to have a big celebration for your birthday," or, "This summer we'll go to Disneyland."

But when promises repeatedly fail to be kept (like when the parent promises never to drink again but ends up sprawled in a heap of empty bottles two weeks later), those pretty words lose their meaning. The child learns that words are one thing but what actually happens is another. With enough repetition of that sort of experience, unpredictability and unreliability become the entire basis of your relationship with your parents. The future always seems uncertain, and that creates anxiety and concern.

Such chronic uncertainty and disappointment can develop into a long-term mistrust of other people. Someone who has been let down, cheated, and manipulated enough times may have trouble trusting even a healthy environment or situation or identifying it in the first place. Other people's good intentions may not seem convincing to him. He may be well-liked, good at his job, respected as a person, but he still feels as if he can never let down his guard. "She *says* she likes me," he thinks, "but why should I believe her?"

If you grew up in a home run by someone with an alcohol addiction, some or all of this might sound familiar to you. To you, the topsy-turvy rules of the alcoholic household may once have seemed—maybe even still seem—like business as usual, rather than something exotic and dysfunctional and negative. It is time for you to see that more clearly.

Giving It a Name

In this book, you will encounter a term that may be new to you: *mentalization*. It refers to something found in a healthy home but often not found in homes burdened by alcohol problems. As a result, it may apply to some of the very things you find hardest to do.

The psychologist behind the concept, Peter Fonagy, described mentalizing as "holding mind in mind."

To put it most simply, mentalization is about understanding yourself and others. It is about your ability to sense your own and others' mental states and to form realistic impressions of those states. You mentalize when you try to understand what motivates you or someone else to act in a particular way, what wishes, thoughts, feelings, and intentions lie behind your behavior and reactions and those of others.

Mentalization encompasses three different aspects. First is your ability to see yourself from the outside, how your behavior looks to and affects the people around you. Second is your ability to understand yourself, why you act and react as you do. It is based on being able to *feel* and to examine your own feelings, thoughts, motivations, and desires. Finally, mentalization has to do with your ability to understand what motivates *other* people's behavior.

The ability to mentalize is something we develop throughout our lives, and you may be good at some aspects of it and not so good at others. It can happen spontaneously, automatically, but it can also be a more intentional and controlled process, when you consciously reflect on an occurrence you may not understand—something you have done or someone else has—and try to analyze it. Either way, in order to navigate the world of people, it is crucial that you be able to mentalize. It is the foundation of meaningful, lasting relationships, enabling you to see the world from the other person's viewpoint while retaining your own stable and confident sense of self.

There's no understanding other people without understanding yourself. This often boils down to relating their actions to something you have thought or felt in a similar situation. That does not mean you have to agree with them, only that you need a sense of what motivates what they say and do. When we fail to mentalize and fail to express our thoughts and feelings in words, we risk misjudging others, which can lead to misunderstandings and conflict, even break-ups and violence.

In an adult, a poorly developed ability to mentalize can express itself in various ways. A poor mentalizer is locked in her own thoughts and feelings, taking them for the only way of perceiving reality when, in fact, they are just one of many. Being imprisoned in that narrow outlook can cause her to bring inappropriate feelings and behaviors to her interactions with other people. In turn, that can generate disappointment and misunderstandings and leave her feeling stranded and isolated, convinced that no one understands her point of view.

Let's say you are someone for whom punctuality is very important, but your partner is running late one day. You take it very personally; as you see it, it represents a lack of love and respect. For some reason, you are reluctant to simply ask your partner what might be behind it, so, nursing your emotional bruise, you go to extremes: You begin to imagine you're no longer loved.

What might you have been told if only you had asked? Your partner probably would have explained exactly what was going on with his day that made him late. He would have reassured you that the lateness had nothing to do with the insult you took it for, and the two of you might have become closer as a result. By honing your mentalization skills, you can learn how to steer clear of possible misunderstandings that can spiral into serious conflict. Think of mentalization like a compass. Without one, a ship is unlikely to reach its destination. Worse still, it stands a good chance of running aground or colliding with other vessels.

"What are they thinking about me as I talk to them, and what will their next move be? Did I go too far with that story I told—too coarse, too honest? I like to make everyone happy, and maybe I'm afraid I'll bore people or offend them. Something inside of me is constantly analyzing, and it exhausts me... With my mind racing so much, I can go a whole evening without being able just to be myself and enjoy the company."—Anna

2

LEARNING TO "HOLD MIND IN MIND"

When you drink, the focus of your thinking processes first shifts from the sensible, analytical part of your brain to the limbic system, where emotions are stored. Inhibitions begin to peel away, and your regard for norms and rules diminishes. That might be fun at first—but you also begin to lose your ability to empathize with other people and to read social signals.

Continue drinking, and the focus eventually descends to the reptilian brain. That's the part of you that concerns itself with sheer survival. This is the stage where you start becoming more "primitive" and your behavior less appropriate—where you lose touch with the possibility that you may be making the people around you uncomfortable.

Someone with an addiction might start off feeling buoyant and unrestrained, both in terms of "good" emotions (ones that may inspire him to try to be as entertaining as possible) and "bad" ones (which may turn him menacing, antagonistic, even violent). Because his mentalization is poor, he misses or blocks out an understanding of how others experience either his giddiness, at the one extreme, or his maliciousness, at the other. Your reptilian brain isn't interested in those subtle distinctions; to it, the world is black and white, and everyone is either your ally or your enemy. That brutal outlook is what you are exposed to if you are in a relationship with someone who has an addiction.

Parents with good mentalizing capabilities are usually good at helping their children develop the same skills. But children who grow up around alcoholism rarely get that kind of support. Powerful censorship can pervade an alcoholic home. There are strict rules about what can and can't be talked about, and they are usually focused on protecting the drinking parent.

If drama and conflict are constantly unfolding around you, but you're not permitted to acknowledge them by talking about them or pointing them out, important connections between what you see and how you feel about it are not allowed to form in your mind. This means the kind of interaction and spontaneity needed for building mentalization skills are absent. Without childhood practice at saying what you feel, at testing what you see against your natural reactions, you may find it difficult even in adulthood to express yourself and understand social situations.

"There were many unwritten rules that we all knew and tried to follow as best we could: Sit up straight! Eat properly! Do your homework! Get good grades! Be polite! Set the table! Serve him first! No laughing at the table! Clean up the mess! Outwardly, we let on as if there were no problems. It was never mentioned, and Dad was allowed to keep up appearances as the sociable, extroverted professional man with a good family life."—Mona

In mentalization-impaired families, parents are often dismissive of their children's feelings. After all, a child's emotions and reactions risk making a parent feel guilty about her drinking, and that's something she is determined to avoid. Even for a child to be in a bad mood may be interpreted by the parent as a direct criticism. The parent might respond with, "Go to your room, and don't come back till you've gotten rid of that sour face!" or, "Don't tell me you're crying again? What's the problem *this* time?"

The child ends up drawing the worst possible conclusions from this repeated scenario. He concludes that his feelings are not okay, that his emotions are something shameful—that there is something inherently wrong with him.

Opening the Channels

To understand others, you must first understand yourself and be able to articulate your thoughts and feelings. Self-awareness doesn't stop at *self*; it is also meant to open up honest channels between you and others. Without a genuine understanding of yourself, you cannot engage in genuine, rewarding interaction with others.

It seems as if understanding and communicating with others ought to be easy, right? Look how alike we are in so many ways: We all need to connect with other people and have meaning in our lives, we share similar physical needs, we all have the capacity to feel joy, sadness, anger, surprise, shame, disgust, and fear. We all are able to imagine, at least in some small way, what it might be like to be someone else, to put ourselves in their place and understand what makes them act and think the way they do, even if we don't seem to be on quite the same wavelength as they are.

But in fact, meaningful dialogue and exchange with others requires a certain amount of skill and, again, honesty. If you are hoping for someone to communicate with you on a serious level, bringing their genuine self to the conversation, you must bring yours as well: If you expect *them* to really be *them*, *you* must really be *you*.

This means tuning in to how you express yourself. Do you do it in a way that renders your feelings transparent, or are you in the habit of camouflaging your thoughts and feelings instead, just as your family did when you were growing up? Do you expect other people to be straightforward with you when perhaps you don't meet that standard yourself?

Take a look at the following and see if any of it applies to how you interact with others.

1. *Reluctance to ask questions.* This is often rooted in the feeling that there is something you ought to understand but don't or embarrassment at revealing it. Or maybe you don't ask because you are afraid of what you might be told. Do you worry that your question could stir up chaos or confusion or lead to you being pushed away, rejected, or shamed?
2. *Feelings of uncertainty about your own judgments, which can make it difficult to set boundaries.* When you are accustomed to always setting aside your own needs, wishes, and feelings and instead taking responsibility for those of others, you may have difficulty managing your own feelings—worrying about how other people feel, to the point that it gets in the way of your own feelings and your ability to make good choices for yourself, puts you at risk. For example, you might feel reluctance or guilt due to a fear of hurting or disappointing someone, and this doubt causes you to do things that you don't want to do, or that may not be appropriate for you.
3. *Initial faith in people that quickly turns to mistrust once they express their thoughts or feelings.* Maybe you believe that talk is cheap and that there will always be a big gap between what someone says and how they

really feel. After all, in your childhood home, you saw that happen again and again.
4. *Believing that you know other people's needs and motives, maybe even better than they do, and that your analysis of the other person is correct—leaving them no room for their own interpretation and experience.* Do you find yourself constantly trying to figure out what's *really* going on under the surface of every conversation, to keep a step ahead of others' feelings and reactions? Are you basing your expectations of them on your own outlook, rather than opening yourself to vibrant and open interaction? Do you try too hard to pick up every possible signal but without asking questions and respecting boundaries? You may be so caught up in your own viewpoint that your assumptions about other people don't leave any room for learning, correction, and growth.
5. *Excessive talking in a way that is out of touch with your feelings and environment.* Talking nonstop has a way of obscuring the fact that you are not in real contact with either yourself or the person you are speaking to. What's more, it often confuses or bores people. Perhaps you are also prone to assuming an authoritative tone on topics that you actually know very little about. This is *pseudomentalization*, a kind of obliviousness as if your behavior were a movie that rolls on and on without taking anyone else—or even your genuine self—into account. Pseudomentalization can camouflage the emptiness and meaninglessness that you may feel underneath.

When mentalization fails, when it breaks down, the result can be conflict—even to the point of violence—separation, and other traumatic situations, not to mention simple insecurity and unpleasant moods. In families shaped by alcohol, such breakdowns occur often, sometimes triggered by minor incidents but then escalating into serious conflagrations. And it doesn't only happen to the person with the addiction (regardless of whether he or she is drunk or sober); everyone in the family is susceptible.

Making conscious changes in the way you communicate is easier said than done. One factor that can get in the way of healthy, honest interaction with others is the "triggers" we will discuss in Chapter 5, which can load your communication with stress. Let's say some unexpected element of a situation resurrects a familiar old feeling of being undervalued or unheard. Suddenly, the center of your thinking shifts from the thoughtful, analytical cortex to your reptilian brain and its survival instincts. The emotional atmosphere around the conversation completely changes, and so does your perception of the other person.

Your brain, unfortunately, may not be good at sorting out whether a perceived threat is large or small, or whether it is even real. Any situation resembling an experience in which you were injured, abandoned, or threatened can put your body on high alert, and from there, you are left with three primal options: *freeze*, *flee*, or *fight*.

Freezing means you are unable to speak, your thought processes grind to a halt, and you feel incapable of acting. *Fighting* does not necessarily mean literal combat—you may begin to yell or turn the conversation in an overly intense or antagonistic direction. *Fleeing* means that you withdraw, physically and/or mentally. You may minimize the importance of the situation or deny there was even a problem, but in one way or another, even by going to sleep, you will make yourself unavailable.

The shock of losing control in a triggering situation can provoke anxiety, and that may upset or embarrass you afterward. In the long run, getting trapped time after time in the same seemingly unavoidable response is exhausting, and it can affect your sense of how you affect your surroundings and your ability to read signals and feel empathy. This can turn allies into enemies.

Mentalization Gone Wrong

Children from a home with alcohol problems are always scrambling, trying to guess what's going on and how they should respond to it. They lack the inner compass that would help them determine where they really belong and what their role is.

When a person constantly tries to keep ahead of others' feelings and reactions, it is called *hypermentalizing*. This is a sort of distorted mentalizing that serves as a defense mechanism against the chaos and unpredictability you are immersed in. A hypermentalizing child will work overtime trying to solve the family's problems: *What could I do so Dad wouldn't have to go out drinking? How can I get Mom and Dad to talk to each other again?*

None of this is based on a genuine understanding of his parents, but without the benefit of the clarity that good mentalizing would have provided, it's the best he can do. He tries hard to pick up on the appropriate signals, but as a child in a home with alcohol abuse, he wasn't trained to do this, and his efforts will never get beyond guesswork.

The ability to mentalize comes from being in a relationship with a caregiver who is able to mentalize themselves. An adult who did not develop that skill in childhood may be at risk of developing certain kinds of distorted perceptions. They might, for example, *hyper*mentalize, considering themselves good at sensing other people's needs and feelings but without real justification for that confidence. Frequently, they get it wrong, drawing conclusions that relate only to their own experiences and not to other people's. They're accustomed to trying to discern others' motives—a survival mechanism they cultivated in their childhood household—but with the mentalizing element absent from their childhood, good instincts regarding personal interaction were not developed. Many simply never learned how to put themselves in the shoes of another person, and consequently, adult children of alcoholics are often not particularly good at understanding their partners.

Childhood hypermentalizing patterns can replay themselves in adulthood, often in relationships where you feel you have a lot at stake. If you suffered from the frequent inaccessibility of a parent, for example, you might be especially sensitive to what seems like similar behavior by someone you now look up to and want acknowledgment from, such as your boss. This can activate a fear that something is wrong with you and leave you agitatedly trying to figure out what you could do to make her like you.

In short, these conditions can linger long after the conditions that bred them. You may have a parent who doesn't drink anymore, but chances are you can still detect the mentalizing problems that resulted from their drinking years. It may be disappointing to discover that, even without the alcohol, your mother still seems to take little interest in you. This illustrates that mentalizing is not static; in order to grow, it needs a continuously stimulating environment. Sadly, relationships can't start functioning healthily until mentalizing occurs. Your parent's drinking put that process on hold for a long time, and reawakening it can take some time.

But the ability to mentalize is something you can consciously develop, and making that effort will mean a great deal to your interactions with others at all levels of intimacy, as well as your overall health and well-being. Think of the following exercises as your first steps toward understanding both yourself and others better.

EXERCISES: CHANGE YOUR THOUGHTS

To develop your mentalizing ability, start by changing your way of thinking. This applies especially if you are someone whose mind seems overactive, running around in circles and dwelling on worries and negative thoughts. If these kinds of nagging concerns do not get resolved, they can wear you down and take a toll on your self-esteem.

The exercises here center on the idea of talking about your ruminations to someone you trust. Choose this person with care, and be sure not to pick, for example, a mother who drinks or a father who is trapped in denial. This person can be someone you already know, as long as you trust them implicitly, and you know them to be good at mentalizing. If you do not feel that your personal circle includes someone like that, it may be necessary to seek help from a professional.

The next time you notice your mind starting to wander in a negative, hyperactive way—perhaps even after that has gone on for a few hours—make a conscious effort to bring the frenetic activity to a halt. Begin by determining whether what you are worried about is something you have any control over. If not, visualize putting those troubling thoughts on a shelf as a way to return to the present moment and put your mind at rest. Thoughts are only thoughts, and they don't necessarily reflect reality. Imagine bundling up all the ones that have bothered you recently and setting them on that shelf, where you will keep them until you have someone to talk with about them.

Now, make your appointment with the person you designated as the one you can trust. Tell your listener about your bundle of thoughts and imagine taking it down from the shelf and opening it. Let your listener help provide you with a reality check.

Without attaching your own interpretation to them, describe the situations or circumstances that have troubled you. Distinguish as best you can between your own interpretation and what objectively played out—you don't want to shade the subject with your own agenda or narrow the range of possible alternative perspectives on it. Keep in mind that it may be less important to recount each and every worry than to try and pinpoint the situation that triggered your unease in the first place.

Once you've told the story in as neutral a manner as possible, then *you can introduce your interpretation, associations, etc. Describe the worst possible outcome, as you picture it, of the situation that has you agitated. It's often your worst fear that determines whether you end up fruitlessly ruminating on a problem, but identifying that fear will let you look it in the eye and decide whether it is even real. Acknowledge your fear—doing that is always illuminating. The fact that it may no longer be a necessary or realistic worry may be the very reason it's worth examining.*

Be aware of your body as you tell your story. Perhaps you get a lump in your throat, your heart starts to race, or you feel a heaviness in your chest or abdomen. Do you recall any situations in which you had the same sensations? Register those feelings (for the moment, you don't need to do anything more with them than that).

Pace your story, taking breaks as you speak. Learning to mentalize involves practicing at becoming more and more precise. Try to develop your story by being as honest as possible. Practice not losing yourself in a thousand details that may tire out your listener or drive you off-topic. Stick to the subject and listen to what you are saying: Make sure it makes sense and can be understood.

And remember: You are interesting. *Many who grew up in homes with alcohol abuse have far too much experience with frustrating conversations, attempted discussions that were interrupted or derailed. Too much of that can leave you believing that neither you nor what you have to say is of any genuine interest. Don't believe it!*

Since you have gone to the trouble of finding someone trustworthy to talk with, uphold your end of the bargain by listening to what they have to say about what you've told them. Their assessment of how realistic your fears are can help steady you and bring your own subjective impressions down to earth.

Afterward, sit down and write about what went through your mind as you spoke. How does it feel to have revealed your thoughts and feelings to someone else? If they have been changed in any way by expressing them out loud to another person, by all means, make a record of it.

These exercises are meant to help you get better at observing your thoughts and feelings as if from the outside. Remember that they represent your interpretation *of reality in the moment, not objective truth. The moment you stop insisting that your own version of reality is simply the way things* are, *rather than a set of conclusions you've drawn from what you experienced personally, the merry-go-round of nagging, self-defeating thoughts will begin to slow down. Regulating your feelings will become easier, and you will have an easier time talking to the sorts of wise, warm people who can lead you to more life-affirming insights.*

As you develop your ability to mentalize, you will also get better at determining whether the things that worry you are things you have the power to change. If so, you'll find you have more courage to act; if not, you can direct your energy toward consciously letting them go.

3

TELLING YOUR OWN STORY

You may not have been aware of it, but we are all constantly creating our own story, even if we are more conscious of it at some times than at others. We do this to ensure that our lives have an inner logic and consistency.

Growing up in a home with addiction problems can get in the way of formulating a healthy story; it can leave your story riddled with troublesome gaps. You may have found it difficult to put your story into words because there was little or no serious discussion of your day-to-day experiences at home. Or you may have found that the words didn't align with your experience, and the discrepancy left you mistrustful of words and stories, whether yours or other peoples' (including your family's).

But the more of your history that you can piece together, the more coherent your personal story will be, and the more coherence and continuity you'll create between your past, your present, and your future.

Connecting the Dots in Your Own Way

When you set out to work on your story, you open up the possibility of understanding the relationship between the child you were and the father or mother you felt you could never reach. You begin to understand your role in your family, which helps you to connect your childhood with your present and learn why you act and react as you do.

Once you embark on this exploration, you begin to see behind the old mirrors, see through the stories your parents told you about yourself. A deeper personal truth emerges about what you saw, felt, and experienced. Keep in mind that the *you* that takes shape may not quite be the person you imagined yourself to be. It may be someone who is, say, naturally happier than you were allowed to be or someone who's not so quiet and timid by nature after all.

You may find that your parents' voices still play inside you, influencing your decisions. Those voices may have been directing you all your life, and the idea of going against what they say triggers feelings of fear and guilt. Your job is to find your *own* voice and develop the skill to identify your *own* values and feelings, and formulate your *own* opinions. Your parents' thoughts, opinions, and admonitions need no longer be a part of your inner soundtrack, and you must learn to overrule them. You can't base your life on the words of someone else, particularly someone who may well have been drunk when they said them.

You cannot change the past events, but you can change the way you move through the world right now, and one way to do that is by reformulating the story you carry around inside you. Make it your objective to create a picture of a clear-headed self, one strong and independent enough to make his or her own choices and decisions.

Sharing Your Story

One way to begin altering your personal story is by doing a course of therapy or group treatment for people who grew up in homes shaped by addiction. Others whose stories are similar to yours may be in a position to provide deep understanding and recognition of your situation. That sort of understanding may be something you've never experienced before, at least not to the extent that you needed it. Seeing your childhood experience validated like that can help you come to grips with how you really feel about it.

When other people truly listen and put themselves in your shoes, when they "mirror" your story, it adds clarity to your view of it. Mirroring is important for the formation of our personality. We can't develop healthily without some sympathetic feedback from our environment.

There is also a lot to be gained by sharing with people who *don't* have the same problems as you. You may know people who seem to have nicely balanced lives and are comfortable with themselves, for whom saying either yes or no comes easily. They may be good at self-expression and have varied, vibrant, and colorful stories to tell about themselves. A lot can be learned from them. Comparing the way you tell your story with the way they tell theirs may give you a clearer perspective on those areas where you are out of balance, where you're prone to anxiety and uncertainty. In the very same areas, they may appear mature and secure, and that can enhance your sense of context.

To Change Your Story Is to Change Your Life

"I have let go of the desire to get my childhood and youth back. Now I am an adult, and four-year-old Annette is either under my wing, or we are walking hand in hand." —Annette

Your well-being as an adult depends on your awareness of your story and on having a vibrant, nuanced, coherent picture of your life. That awareness can be difficult to achieve, and to reach it, you must do the work. This means that, for a time, at least, you will have to come to grips with the pain connected with your upbringing. Don't be surprised if ugly memories bring ugly moods—remind yourself that once you have changed your image of your past, altered your story, much of that ugliness will disappear.

If you do not work with your story, you not only won't relieve your suffering, but you will also run the risk of history repeating itself for you and your loved ones. There is never a guarantee that you won't repeat mistakes your parents made, but you can create other options for yourself, including ways to ensure that you have effective means of repairing the damage if you do falter like that.

You have the ability to take different actions. Because you can see your story more objectively, and because you better understand the consequences of your parents' behaviors, you have a wider choice of action in any given situation.

The whole purpose of increasing your self-understanding is to able to steer your life in the directions most appropriate for you. By working with your story, you get in touch with yourself as you are, learn *why* you are as you are, and take full advantage of your increased understanding of your patterns and reactions. You trace the origins of your wounds, your low self-esteem, your sense of insecurity toward other people. Delving into yourself in that way also enhances your understanding of your parents and siblings.

As your story gets colored in and becomes more nuanced, you mature. The more stories you can tell about your life, the more images you can convey, the richer your self-image will be, and the more substantial your life, both past, and present, will look to you. You will be more *visible* to yourself, whereas the role you previously assigned yourself in your own childhood may have been as a mere bystander.

There are many resources for working toward understanding your story better. Sometimes the work can threaten to overwhelm you with powerful emotions, and at those times, having some kind of therapist to talk with can make a significant difference.

EXERCISES: YOUR HISTORY, YOUR STORY

1. *A Chronology of Your Life*

Create a timeline of your life in which you list, chronologically, all the significant events from your birth until today. These should be events that influenced you and your family, for example, divorce and other crises, moving, changing schools, illness, the beginning of a parent's drinking, when you left home, romantic relationships, marriage, the birth of children, educational degree, jobs, etc. You decide how much detail to include. Enlist the help of family and close friends to help make the timeline as accurate as possible.

The more events you place on your timeline, the better. You may encounter periods when you cannot precisely pinpoint events in time or sequence: Maybe you do not know when you actually moved to a new city and started going to a new school. Filling out the timeline will help you discover where there are gaps in your story.

2. Meaningful People

Create a list of people and even pets that you bonded with during your childhood, the ones you now believe made it possible for you to get through the difficulties of your upbringing. It doesn't matter whether that bonding existed for a short time or a long one.

Include the people you loved and respected, and who loved and respected you, the ones who actually saw you. List the people who were truly there for you in your childhood, rather than the ones you wished had been there more. For example, for your father to appear in this list, it is not enough that he meant a great deal to you if he did not, in fact, spend much time with you. The list must include the people who were there. It may be that the door to your grandmother's home was always open to you, and she loved you unconditionally—maybe her home was a refuge for you. Or maybe a friend's parents fulfilled the same role. A teacher or a mentor at an after-school club or activity whom you could always talk to might also be on your list.

Who was there for you as you grew up? In what ways were they there for you? Add no one to the list who in any way hurt or betrayed you unless they eventually took responsibility, repaired the damage, and built a secure relationship with you. And if you spent long hours in a pet's company because it gave you a feeling of peace and security, include the pet in your list too.

Your list may look something like this:

Grandma: *Her door was always open. We didn't talk about problems, but she was always nice and happy to see me.*

My English teacher Mr. _____: *He treated me with respect and believed in my abilities. He supported me in doing my homework and encouraged me to do my best.*

My friend _____: *We always laughed a lot, and I remember that she once brought me a gift when she came back from a summer trip she took with her family.*

Calling all these people to mind will probably trigger a powerful mix of emotions in you: Love, sadness, longing, gratitude. You may suddenly recall what the world felt like when you were small and dependent on the care of adults and how vulnerable you were. These emotions have great meaning—allow yourself to feel them as you compile your list.

But what if the emotions that surge inside you are primarily grief and anger because it's difficult for you to think of anyone *to put on your list? As painful as it may be if this is your situation,* claim *that pain—your anger is completely justified. There surely must have been adults who could have helped you but looked the other way—honor and credit yourself for going on to make a life despite that disadvantage. You have worked hard and drawn on many inner resources, and you have yourself to thank for getting you through your childhood.*

4

DIFFICULT FEELINGS

If you grew up in a house where emotions were not talked about and expressed in safe ways, you may not only have never learned how to express your feelings, you may not have learned how to recognize them in the first place. They may have been sources of fear and shame when you expressed them, which reinforced your need to keep them shut down.

> "Way too many times, we 'danced Dad's dance' to avoid unpleasant situations. If we sensed he was in a bad mood, we wouldn't ask him about anything for fear of setting him off. When we could tell he wasn't happy, we kept ourselves from laughing, and we tried to laugh on the rare occasion when he showed a sense of humor. We didn't get into conversations with him, so he got his way most all the time."—Mona

Perhaps it is only now that you're getting in touch with your feelings and allowing them to occupy the same room as you rather than being locked away somewhere. That's your starting point: You must consciously work with your feelings, learning to identify them. You must develop a relationship with them. Learn to put them into words, either through therapy or observing people who seem to be in better touch with their feelings than you. It may be difficult for you to believe, but your emotions and theirs are the same—everyone starts with the same basic set. The difference is in how you handle them. If you build up your skill at sensing, identifying, expressing, and accommodating your emotions, the feeling that you are at the mercy of uncontrolled outbursts and overreactions will give way to a sense of control.

No feelings are wrong. Your feelings are okay. Dare to get in touch with them. Dare to learn how to express them in ways that enrich your interactions with the people around you.

All Feelings Are Okay

As we said before, all people are born with the ability to feel and express the same set of primary emotions. We start with six of them—anger, sadness, fear, joy, surprise, and disgust. A seventh, shame, begins to emerge at about age three. Each of these feelings can be experienced to different degrees and given different names. Anger, for example, can be experienced as mere irritation but also as contempt and rage.

Each culture has its own norms and preferences regarding which emotions are permissible to express and how much. The culture we grow up in sets limits on what kinds of feelings we are allowed to show and how we should respond to them. An individual family also has its own ecology related to feelings, much of which tends to reflect the parents' own upbringing. Each of us has received training at home in how to deal with our feelings, but for some of us, that training was in a healthy direction, and for others, it wasn't.

"When there is something good in my life, at work or in private or otherwise, it is challenging for me. I have not really been able to experience pleasure and be happy. Each time, an inner voice

says, 'Don't enjoy it too much—it's too good to be true.'"
—Charlotte

As you investigate your own "emotional ecology," begin by looking for major blockages, disconnections, or confusion you may have around specific emotions. Perhaps you think of yourself as someone who never gets angry. Or maybe you cry when you are angry or pick fights when you are sad. It could be that, in your family, showing anger was not allowed, so you expressed it in these other ways instead. Or perhaps it's hard for you to experience happiness in a sustained way; experiencing one disappointment after another, you learned not to believe in positive, joyful outcomes.

The problem for you now, as an adult, is that your expressions of feeling don't reap the reactions from others that you need or expect. Why? Because you aren't actually signaling your true feelings. You learned long ago to put them through a kind of filter that changes them, as far as other people can tell, into something else. Your own difficulty in recognizing and regulating your emotions sends confusing signals to others and makes it challenging for the outside world to understand you.

Begin "Thawing" Your Emotions

"When things went well for me, or it had been a good night, or a travel experience, or just a nice moment, that moment would quickly be followed by thoughts of some injury about to happen to me. I was not capable of daring to be happy, and especially not good at maintaining joy. My subconscious idea was that if I didn't allow myself to be totally happy, I would be less disappointed."—Anna

Notice if you are protecting yourself from feelings, whether your own or those of others. Do you try to distance yourself from emotions? Do you worry about not being liked because of the emotions you express? Is your opinion of other people influenced by how expressive (or inexpressive) of emotion they are? Watch for ways in which you may isolate yourself from others and consider whether you are motivated by a desire to avoid confronting feelings.

Notice whether you ever think that it is not okay to feel what you are feeling, or if you just don't seem to have certain feelings at all. Perhaps you never cry or get angry. You might think that those same feelings are also not okay when expressed by others. Notice, too, whether you allow your feelings or those of others to become your drama—either by blaming yourself for them or by feeling attacked or wounded by them. You might also find yourself guarding against some form of discomfort, perhaps fear or anxiety or feelings of low self-worth, that leads you to avoid going more deeply into the other emotions that might be underneath.

If you find yourself having difficulty accommodating your emotional pain and that of others, take stock of the confusion that comes with it. When you are unable to be direct about your feelings, the need to get real, underlying emotional needs met may lead to manipulation by you or by the people around you. The cascading confusion that can result can be very difficult to contain.

Depression Caused by Frozen Emotions

Do you often feel something smoldering inside you or have periods in which you feel yourself spiraling downward into a "black hole?" Is it sometimes hard for you to appreciate and take in all the positive input that comes your way, even though your despair makes no logical sense from the outside looking in?

These experiences aren't confined to outcasts or misfits; they can arise even for someone who has a partner, children, and a good job, someone who generally has done well with her life.

Such problems can indicate a kind of depression that comes from frozen emotions. Frozen anger and frozen sadness—and the feelings of powerlessness, disappointment, anxiety, despair, and/or hopelessness that they generate—are natural reactions to unbearable situations you may have faced day in and day out in your formative years.

A large number of adult children of alcoholics take antidepressants at some point in their lives, and they often think of themselves as depressive. *But your depressiveness is not a personality trait.* You may be considered to be depressed by your doctor, but the sort of depression that often haunts families with addiction problems is different from the serious illness of that name that needs to be treated both medically and with talk therapy. You were born with the capacity for all the emotions—they are your birthright as a whole human being—and the frozen feelings can be thawed and set free, the depressiveness released.

Sadness and grief

Deeply repressed grief often lies underneath the depression that may affect families with addiction problems. You may be carrying around a very real sorrow over the lack of good care you received as a child and the resulting complications and limitations that you live with as an adult. Look this grief in the eye: Give yourself permission to grieve as you delve into your feelings of sadness. Allow yourself to cry over the grief you have been carrying for so long. Doing this is not dangerous; facing the grief will not pull you down into some bottomless pit. Instead, you'll find it liberating. The support of a therapist, a friend, someone you trust, so you are not alone when you work through those sad feelings, can be highly valuable.

Anger

By nature, we are born with the ability to defend ourselves, an innate form of aggression. But in situations where boundaries are often never taught and are exceeded both verbally and physically, such as in a family with addiction problems, healthy anger gets suppressed while unhealthy anger is acted out to destructive ends. But anger does not need to become destructive. It is not about lashing out or harming others, but about taking care of ourselves by having healthy boundaries.

The violence associated with unhealthy anger can make it a challenging emotion to thaw. Notice whether you inhibit your own anger as a way to distance yourself from the anger you saw too much of in your parents or other people; it makes sense that, with their outbursts, their destructiveness, and their general ill-temper, you don't want to be like them. When people around you express healthy anger, do you feel yourself falling back into old patterns? Do you get anxious and begin to fear for your safety? Do you brace yourself and wish you could flee the scene?

The fact is that anger can be expressed in a healthy, not dramatic, or destructive way. Notice how and when you are likely to turn anger into a negative feeling rather than a positive one.

By permitting yourself to feel anger and assuring yourself that it can be done safely, you will begin to develop the skill to express it in ways that won't hurt yourself or anyone else.

Leave Drama Behind: Follow the Healthy Feelings that Lead to Authentic Joy

THE DEPENDENT BIORHYTHM

The rhythm of someone with an addiction manifests in rapid mood changes and unpredictable behavior and reactions. By substituting a mood-altering substance for a genuine, close connection with the environment, the person alters his/her mood in an artificial way. The moods of someone with a dependency can seem overdramatic and intense, and out of sync with the actual situation.

THE HEALTHY BIORHYTHM

It is natural to have good and bad spells, and all people's moods change in response to what is happening in their environment. Hormones and thoughts can affect mood, as can the moods of other people and any number of aspects of one's surroundings. Natural changes in mood are responsive and relational, not overdramatic or reactive.

WHAT IS YOUR RHYTHM?

YOU CAN LEARN TO REGULATE YOUR RHYTHM IN DIFFERENT WAYS:

- Spend time with family or good friends
- Devote sufficient attention to essential elements of your life such as laundry and paying bills
- Do relaxing activities such as yoga and meditation
- Go for a walk in nature
- Learn something new and interesting
- Take care of your body's natural needs for sleep, food and touch
- Think positively and constructively

The fact that you have chosen to read this book means you may have concluded that there is a large difference between a healthy emotional landscape and the one you grew up in. The rhythm of a healthy, collective give-and-take of emotions is quite distinct from the often unpredictable and intense mood swings experienced by families with dependencies, as they lurch from problem to problem, chaos to even more chaos, seesawing between over-the-top emotions and a sullen emptiness that seems to lack any emotion at all.

As strange as it sounds, if you have lived most of your life with this kind of emotional intensity, you may not recognize yourself when there are no problems or conflicts bearing down on you. The thought of stillness and tranquility may seem frightening and strange, and your habitual reaction will be to create drama where there isn't any, even to the point of putting your relationships at risk. Take a close look at your behavior to see whether that pattern and rhythm apply to you. Don't confuse the exhausting emotional roller coaster of dependency and entanglement with genuine openness and intimacy and authentic expression of feelings.

A family with a substance abuse problem may ricochet back and forth between an emotional black hole and almost ecstatic joy. Even though that joy is inauthentic and can't be trusted, it can be very effective in helping to suppress whatever genuine feelings lie below the surface. Since those genuine feelings threaten the dependency, pressure develops to maintain that artificial euphoria and avoid facing the facts.

Prolonged exposure to these pendulum swings can leave you constantly expecting either the best or the worst and nothing in between—this charges every expression of feelings with a sense of risk. It can blind you to the possibility of steady, loving relationships that are not explosive and not crippled by blocked emotions.

Changing these patterns is, first, about having the courage to *feel your own feelings*. But it is also about daring to open yourself up to the feelings of others. It is about discovering the authentic joy inside you, your inner sense of gratitude, and transforming it into nourishment for your life and the lives of the people around you. Activities that truly nourish you occupy every category, from the simplest and most practical to the most profound, from spending time with friends to enjoying nature or exercising to paying your bills to doing your laundry. Consciously trying to instill a healthy rhythm in yourself can be hard work, but it comes with a reward: It starts you on the road toward a sense of emotional balance that will let you create something positive.

The more you consciously try to focus on people's positive sides or the positive in any given situation, the more you train your mind and brain to be glad and positive. With your willpower, you can strengthen your ability to see more nuances and positivity in everyday situations. When you do, it activates a positive spiral. It is not just a superficial exercise—you actually nourish yourself with more and more good experiences. You connect with, talk about, and think more about the good, and it changes you. It enables you to do more good.

EXERCISES: BE AWARE OF YOUR FEELINGS

Each of us is born with the capacity for seven primary feelings:

Anger *(irritation, bitterness, opposition, aggression, contempt/hate, rage)*

Sadness *(melancholy, sorrow, despair, grief)*

Fear *(insecurity, nervousness, worry, anxiety, panic)*

Joy *(satisfaction, gratitude, happiness, celebration, love)*

Surprise *(astonishment, amazement, overload, shock)*

Disgust *(displeasure, suffering, aversion, repulsion)*

Shame *(shyness, feeling different from others, awkwardness, embarrassment, guilt, humiliation)*

A person who grew up in a family with substance abuse may have learned to suppress certain feelings and avoid expressing them. As a result, the sudden surfacing of those forbidden emotions can trigger anxiety and discomfort in you. You may find yourself wanting to banish them because they don't fit into the image of yourself that you are accustomed to and worked so hard to create. But feelings do not disappear—if you are to be your whole self and abandon your old patterns, they must be felt, lived, and worked through.

1. Emotional Diary

Every day for about two weeks, write down the feelings you've experienced over the course of the day and what triggered them. Do this to bring greater awareness of what goes on inside you to define and clarify your picture of your emotions. Ask yourself these questions:

Which emotions do I feel safe experiencing, acknowledging, and expressing?

Which feelings do I have trouble experiencing, feeling, and expressing?

Is there a particular feeling that causes me more trouble than others?

(If so, elaborate on it and examine exactly how this plays out. For example, you may feel out of touch with anger, but since anger is something that all humans have the capacity to feel and that we all experience from time to time, your detachment from it means your anger is blocked. There could be any number of reasons for this. Maybe you had a parent who was always angry, or you were taught to suppress your anger. Either one of those scenarios could have left you unsure of how anger should really feel and how you should handle it. This needs serious exploration. To start discovering your anger, begin by noticing what irritates you. (Irritation is a form of anger.)

The more primary emotions, such as anger, that you have problems with, the more important it is to start working consciously to identify them, accommodate/allow them, and express each one appropriately.

It is fundamental and necessary for you to be in contact with your feelings. They help you orient toward others and toward your own values. You need to learn to differentiate them from each other and learn how to control how you express and show them in different situations. It takes practice to be able to modulate your feelings up or down. It takes time and the desire on your part to achieve control over the expression of your feelings so that they don't just hit you like a bolt of lightning out of a clear blue sky. There is a reason for every feeling you have.

By writing a feelings journal over the next two weeks, you will achieve valuable and necessary self-awareness. That can take work—don't expect to be able to sleepwalk your way through it. But without that awareness, you will continue to live with the frozen emotions, blocked feelings, and dysfunctional ways of dealing with feelings that pervaded your family's home, and they will continue to create pain, conflict, and misunderstanding. Greater awareness of them will also give you more wisdom in determining how much room to allow them to occupy in your life.

Having at least the beginnings of that awareness is essential to doing the rest of the work in this book.

2. Explore the Seven Primary Feelings

For each of the seven emotions—anger, sadness, fear, joy, surprise, disgust, and shame—answer the following questions.

1) In what situations do you get _____ (angry, etc.)? Is there a particular context or situation in which that emotion is most likely to arise?

2) How does your body feel when you experience (anger, etc.) _____ ?

3) How do you speak to others about your feeling of _____ ?

4) Can you remember how your parents reacted when you felt _____ ?

In your work with registering and experiencing the different feelings you have, it will be valuable to try to understand what creates the feelings. Try to understand the connection between your feelings and what might have triggered them. • Be aware of the situations that make you feel this feeling. Does it remind you of something in particular?

If there are feelings you don't feel at all or feelings you do not know how to express, there is work for you to do.

You must start to feel and express your feelings. For example, if you cannot feel angry but realize that you can often feel annoyed, or you often get into discussions with people when you think you might have been quite upset with the one you discussed with, then you will be able to spot the anger by sitting down when you are alone with yourself or when you talk to a good friend about that. Try to keep on focusing on the irritation and "take the elevator down." During the irritation, you will often feel anger or maybe sadness.

3. How did your family respond to emotions?

*What was your family's typical reaction to each of the different emotions, and how did it affect you? Write down specific examples that come to mind. Begin with **anger** (irritation, bitterness, opposition, aggression, contempt/hate, rage). For example, "Only my father was allowed to be angry, and he was angry* *most of the time," or, "My mother had huge fits of rage, but a long time would pass between them."*

Then carry on with the other six:

Sadness *(melancholy, sorrow, despair, grief)*

Fear *(insecurity, nervousness, worry, anxiety, panic)*

Joy *(satisfaction, gratitude, happiness, celebration, love)*

Surprise *(astonishment, amazement, overload, shock)*

Disgust *(displeasure, suffering, aversion, repulsion)*

Shame *(shyness, feeling different from others, awkwardness, embarrassment, guilt, humiliation)*

4. Connect with Your Feelings

You are born with the ability to experience all sorts of feelings, and they are yours. You can use your feelings to make good decisions with consideration for yourself. You can use your feelings to decide who you want to be with and who you should not be with. You can use your feelings to be good to yourself. Being aware of your feelings is essential. Being rejected because of something you feel is experienced as the ultimate rejection. You are not your emotions, but your emotions are an expression by/of you in the moment, and it is meaningful to examine them. It is important to allow yourself to experience all sorts of emotions. Expressing all *your feelings is not always appropriate—it depends on the situation. But it is important to have the courage to face all your feelings and understand how different events are impacting you emotionally right now.*

5. Learn to Modulate Your Feelings and Emotions

Learning to regulate feelings and emotions can be a lifelong challenge. Feelings don't all share the same intensity: Each one falls at a different place on a continuum, ranging from very subtle to very powerful. Teaching yourself to modulate your expression of them will give you more control over how they affect yourself and others.

Imagine that you have a volume dial for each of the primary emotions we identified at the beginning of the chapter. Your objective is to learn to use each of those dials. Sometimes it is necessary to boost one of the emotions, and at other times you need to be able to turn one down. But you were not born with this ability. No one is. A child needs the help of adults to develop this skill.

High-intensity emotional states are generally stressful, so it is especially important to learn to handle feelings that are pitched at extreme levels. On the other side of that coin, in situations in which you either register too little emotion or simply don't feel it, you may leave yourself inadequately protected or acknowledged —you give the people around you no way of knowing how you really feel. The overall lesson is that you must get a firm grasp on those volume dials and learn to turn them in both *directions, as needed.*

When emotions need to be dialed back

When you have the sensation of being flooded by a feeling such as anger, to the point that you can barely think clearly or you want to destroy something or strike someone, then that feeling has clearly gone too far; it has become too intense. In that state, you run a high risk of doing some kind of permanent damage.

Recognize that in circumstances like those, you need to turn that volume dial down.

To help you develop your control over such situations, it's a good idea to prepare a list of thoughts and activities that normally have a calming effect on you. If you find your emotions overheating, begin by saying soothingly to yourself, "I can handle this; it will be okay," and then start working your way through your prepared list. Augment your list with the following simple mental and physical actions:

- *Count slowly backward from 10 (or higher) to 1, breathing very slowly as you count.*
- *Mentalize; Put yourself in the other person's shoes by seeking a good explanation for their behavior rather than jumping to a negative, judgmental analysis. "My child is just a toddler, and he's not behaving this way because he wants to hurt me. It's because he's tired and needs a nap."*
- *See your feelings as a reaction to one of your own thoughts, rather than to some absolute reality. Step back from your feelings to get a more inclusive, bird's-eye view of what is happening.*
- *Drink a glass of water in sips, focusing on the feel of the water in your mouth, throat, and stomach.*
- *No matter how out-of-place it may feel, try* smiling. *This will send a little dose of positive information to your brain.*
- *Do some of the exercises from this book, such as the grounding exercise in Chapter 7 or the angel exercise in Chapter 9.*
- *Jump! Go for a walk! Run a lap around your house! All these things can help dislodge anger from your body.*

- *Get in touch with nature in any way you know how.*
- *Talk to someone you are comfortable with—someone you know is good at mentalizing.*
- *If all else fails, leave the situation; take a break. Set a time to revisit it later.*

When emotions need to be intensified

When you do not respond to being poorly treated, when you do not speak up about what you want—or maybe even know *what you want or what is important to you—then boosting that volume dial is important. Look for cues that you haven't given enough attention to certain situations and make a mental note to return to them when you are better at regulating your feelings. Those situations will probably still be unfinished, on hold as they wait for you to resolve them.*

Turning up your feelings can involve both physical and mental activities and sensations. Here are some pathways for enlivening them:

- *Engage in exercise that builds strength and boosts your heart rate.*
- *Formulate affirmations that focus on your innate worth and your rights. Encourage yourself to feel and express feelings with more intensity.*
- *Speak to yourself supportively and appreciatively as if you were your own best friend.*
- *Look for role models and try to emulate them.*
- *Firm up your grasp of the reality of a particular situation by talking about it with people you trust.*
- *If, on some occasions, your feelings seem more vivid than usual, take note of it. Ask yourself why—what helped intensify those feelings for you? If you can*

pinpoint some particular cause, work at getting conscious control over it so you can employ it whenever you need it. Visualize the desired effects and picture yourself deliberately bringing them about. And reward yourself in some way afterward.

6. Smile Every Day

Begin every day with a smile. Some studies show that smiling—just that little movement of your mouth—promotes noradrenaline and serotonin production in the brain. These are chemicals that increase feelings of joy and love. If you find it difficult, put a picture or some kind of memento, something that brings joy and good memories, on your nightstand or on a wall where you will see it upon waking. And smile.

Set a goal of smiling at least once a day at someone you do not know. The purpose is not to get that person to smile back, even though that would be a positive thing. Rather, this little act of faith will help make room for happiness inside you.

EXERCISE: WRITE YOUR LIFE STORY

Childhood, Part 1

Every chapter in this workbook is followed by exercises that are specifically related to that chapter's subject. But, beginning here and for the following nine chapters, each chapter will also include one step in a bigger and much more ambitious project: to write the story of your life.

At the end of Chapter 3, you created a timeline of significant events in your life, from your birth to the present day. That time-

line is now going to serve as a road map as you chronicle your own history.

There is no fixed template for this story; you decide how much detail to include. And of course, just as in your actual life, you won't be the story's only character. Make a point of including the people listed in the previous exercise's "Meaningful People" list, for example.

There is no right or wrong way to begin—how about telling what you know about the day you were born? This exercise is about putting your whole life story into a coherent narrative. If there are events or situations that you do not remember, ask family members or friends, if possible. A chat with a sober parent, for example, may reveal things about you as a child that you weren't aware of.

This is a big project; there's no doubt about it, but there is no deadline for finishing it. And although you may not feel up to the task just yet, there are advantages to getting started now. This book aims to engage you in the process of becoming aware of your feelings, of those feelings' origins in your childhood, and of the influence they have had on you as an adult. If you read the book and craft your story at the same time, the reading will enhance and illuminate the writing, and vice versa.

That's why "Write Your Life Story" has been broken down into smaller, manageable parts. Don't stew over how much time or effort you will require to complete the whole thing—focus on just one section at a time, and take breaks as needed. It may take several months to get it all down. And be aware that there will be sections that are hard to write and painful to get through; those may take longer than others.

But your efforts will bring rewards. Once you've written about some of the hardest things, the heavy emotions and the events you most want to forget, you will find that you have released them from some dark, heavy place inside you. Some people describe this process as making room for lighter, less frightening feelings.

Most importantly, once you put what has burdened you and caused you pain into black-and-white, it becomes easier to see that you and those dark feelings are not the same things. *You have experienced them, but they are not your identity. You are* you; *you may have experienced a betrayal or an abandonment that no one took responsibility for or managed, but you no longer have to allow that to determine who you are.*

Take whatever practical steps are necessary to make this project easier and more comfortable. Keep a notepad and pen within easy reach at all times, or leave the file open on your computer so you can sit down and add to it at any time. It need not occupy more than 15 minutes a day if that's as much time as you can spare.

The sections will be in chronological order, chapter by chapter, and each section features a set of questions or prompts to help guide your writing.* However, you are not obliged to write them in that order (there may be parts you are more or less interested in at first or know more or less about), and issues may come to mind that the questions don't cover. Remember, this is your *story.*

Let the following prompts and questions guide you as you write this first part of your life story.

Describe yourself as a child.

What was it like growing up and being a child in your family? Were things predictable or unpredictable? What was the general mood? Was it safe? Was it uneasy? Was the atmosphere secure, negative, nice, comfortable?

How did your parents behave when they had conflicts? How did you talk with each other when there was trouble? Was there silence, blame, and accusatory drama? Quarrels, violence, isolation, or sensible talk? Did you get positive recognition or only scolding?

It's time to get started!

5

EMOTIONAL TRIGGERS

Our history often determines how we react emotionally in our relationships. Some couples therapists even postulate that 90 percent of our behavior comes from our past experiences. If your upbringing was problematic, you might continually encounter difficult situations that are rooted in that past. It is important to recognize just how influential a role your background plays in situations where you find yourself overreacting in anger, feeling anxious, or just plain getting bogged down.

A traumatic background can leave you with what are called *triggers*. These are a sort of booby trap that, when activated, causes you to react to a given situation more dramatically than the situation seems to warrant. The cause of it may not be a particular traumatic experience, but rather patterns of behavior that you internalized during your childhood. A trigger will gather very strong feelings around it, feelings of pain, discomfort, and exaggerated sensitivity, and charge them with such intensity that your reactions are excessive—you lose your center.

For example, picture a situation where your children are not listening to you or are not responding. It's really only a minor bother, but it makes you furious, and you fly off the handle for some reason. Why? Rewinding to your own childhood, you are reminded that your parents never seemed to hear what you said to them; they never listened to you. This left you feeling unworthy and unimportant, as if your voice didn't matter. Even all these years later, you continue to hold that feeling inside you, and when you find yourself confronting a stubborn five-year-old, the accumulated old feelings trigger an unreasonable reaction. It makes that part of you oversensitive and more vulnerable to stress than the rest of you.

There is a wide variety of potential triggers, and it can be confusing to see yourself, generally an agreeable person who is well-liked and seems to manage fine as an adult, suddenly, unexplainably, explode and act like a child. In a split-second, you can find yourself in a living hell.

Become Aware of Your Triggers

To begin developing your awareness of your own triggers, think back on the last situation in which you overreacted. When was the last time you felt as if the rug was being pulled out from under you, and your feelings threatened to engulf you? (One indication of this kind of situation may be that you felt embarrassed about it afterward.)

Acknowledging that you are prone to these episodes—cursing at your children or exploding with anger at your partner—may be difficult. After all, that is behavior that we generally consider *not okay*, and you may be left with a guilty conscience. But the causes go deep, and you must try to get to the story behind it all. If you examine them honestly, your triggering episodes will begin to reveal patterns, and those will help tell you what you need to know.

Emotional outbursts are not the only possible effect of triggering. You may experience anxiety instead or to go into a "freeze" mode. A mild form of criticism, for example, may suddenly plunge your self-esteem into a bottomless pit, or you may find yourself lying awake at night, agitated when there is not really anything to worry about.

Learning to calm yourself and stop the loss of control starts with identifying your trigger points. You must get back to their root cause. Think of it as letting them tell their story. Once you have uncovered the reason behind them, being triggered will no longer be something that happens out of the blue with no explanation. Realizing that you have vulnerability in a certain area, you can take measures to help prevent it from getting the best of you—the next time your children are not listening to you, you will find it easier to catch yourself before you react too intensely. It will be obvious that the dramatic surge of energy inside you is not quite called for. You will see that it is your *story* talking, not really *you*.

Developing awareness of your triggers and what's behind them will have a significant impact on your life. It will enable you to consider the big picture when something causes you a problem. In the case of a screaming child, for instance, rather than thinking she's being uncooperative merely to irritate you, you might open your mind to other possibilities: she's tired; she wants to go home; her friend has a pair of shoes that she thinks are nicer than her own; she's investigating how much power she has and how much influence she has on her life situation; she can't quite regulate her feelings, and she shows them to you because she is dependent on you and confident that you'll take care of it.

If you view the situation through the eyes of your history, you may, in your mind, find yourself replacing the actual characters

—the adult you and your little child—with your mother and yourself as a child, in a problematic relationship. If that happens, there's a risk of an unhappy history repeating itself.

Such trigger points are a great burden because every time they run away with you, they eat away at your self-esteem and open the door to self-hatred. That is why it is crucial to spot them and examine them. You need the kind of understanding of them that will let you put on the brakes before things have gone too far. What was it, exactly, in your child's behavior that made you angry? Was your interpretation of it accurate, or was it skewed by some unfortunate story from your past?

Tackling your triggers and getting control over your behavior is a step-by-step process, and it is based on the insights that questions like these bring. It also allows you to feel those feelings, even if they seem frightening. Facing up to them is a key step in the path toward being able to say, "This reaction is a trigger point talking; it's not something horribly, irreversibly wrong with me." A sense of calm will come over you more easily if you can assure yourself that an overreaction is not your whole being falling to pieces but rather a single trouble spot that needs your close and loving attention. Have compassion for yourself: Tell yourself that you are who you should be but that you have some troublesome areas that you would like to change. Each of those areas has its own revealing story to tell.

Watch for these typical reactions to trigger points:

- A sudden, radical emotional change from one moment to another with emotion that is out of proportion to the situation. The way you perceive a given situation may suddenly change. You may experience it as if you are "frozen." Rage/anger/contempt may bubble up inside

you, giving you the feeling that the rug is being pulled out from under your feet.
- A bodily reaction of some sort. Your heart starts pounding, and you can feel the blood coursing through your arms and legs. Or maybe the tone of your voice suddenly changes and becomes cold and sharp.
- Mentalizing breakdown. You feel rigid and less able to express yourself, unable to see the situation from any perspective but your own. Your body language becomes more aggressive, and your speech becomes rough and tense.
- You close yourself off from what is happening around you. You feel shame.

EXERCISE: YOUR TRIGGER POINTS

Think back on the last three months and try to recall times when you felt an inner trigger suddenly activated. Keep in mind that you likely have more than one kind of trigger, and it is important to identify and work through all of them. If it helps, write down your answers to these questions:

What happened in this situation?

What went through your mind as it began to happen?

If it seemed to be caused by a particular person, what specifically did that person do?

What unmet needs may have been behind your strong reaction?

Did the feelings aroused in you seem familiar from previous situations?

What do you wish had happened instead?

There is always a story behind every situation that triggers an emotional overreaction, either from your adult life or childhood. At first, you may not recall that story, but the longer you work with these questions, the likelier it is that the story will finally reveal itself. This kind of internal work is especially important if your children often activate your trigger points—this is about your history, not theirs. You must not allow them to suffer for difficulties you had long before they were born.

Even though maintaining your equilibrium in triggering situations will get easier as you develop your awareness of your trigger points, you may actually find yourself with increased sensitivity to certain situations. But your new awareness will change the way you relate to them. In general, making a connection with a therapist can be very helpful. Regardless of the specifics of your situation, though, there are techniques that anyone can use to restore calm when stress builds up. A number of these were listed in the previous chapter, and the list below can be considered complementary to those. If possible, try each of the following activities to see what may be helpful for you in triggering situations.

- *Speak to yourself in soothing, comforting, and appreciative ways. Support and care for yourself. Picture speaking to the troubled part of you just as an adult would comfort a scared child.*
- *Seek out good and trusted friends and share your feelings and the stories behind your behavior.*
- *Go for walks in nature.*
- *Listen to music.*
- *Relax in a bath or shower.*
- *Get a hug from your partner or a good friend.*
- *Exercise.*

Be aware that your triggering problems may explain not only your behavior but that of others as well. There may have been a time when your unexpected escalation of a situation drove someone else to react unreasonably or even violently. Do your best to apologize for such situations and try to mend your relationships. You could say—even to your children—that you are sorry that you sometimes get so angry and that you realize it is not okay. Say that you will do everything in your power to stop. In the case of children, remember to take full *responsibility, so the child does not get the idea that your loss of control is somehow his fault.*

EXERCISE: WRITE YOUR LIFE STORY

Childhood, Part 2

Let the questions below guide you as you write the next part of your life story.

How did your parents handle losses and negative experiences such as diseases, accidents, death, divorce, abuse? Was an effort made to heal wounds?

Did you ever feel threatened or rejected by your parents?

Who really took care of you? Who talked to you and gave you support and comfort when you were sad? Who understood your needs as a child?

6

SELF-ESTEEM

None of us is born with self-esteem. It is something that develops through our relationships, especially with the people closest to us. Its development, in one direction or the other, is an ongoing process: It is either strengthening or weakening. Your self-esteem follows you around and influences everything in your life, including friendships, romantic relationships, and relationships in general. It helps determine whether you pursue your interests and choose good things for your life, whether you feel deserving of comfort and success and nourishment. Your self-esteem status can also affect how people behave toward you; it can make the difference between your being treated well or poorly. In short, it means everything to your overall well-being.

"I started to play handball, and I made some friends who came from normal families. It was very confusing for me, but I built up two identities. One was the handball player who went to great effort to hide her family. The other was the nice girl who hung out with some of the cool kids at school, where she didn't have to hide her family. But both identities felt wrong, and I was never quite at home with myself. I was always vigilant and a step

ahead. I was unsure of myself, and although I hid my insecurities behind a strong facade, a hard shell, deep down, I was a frightened child with very poor self-esteem. I felt ugly, fat, and worthless."—Lene

If, when you were a child, it seemed as if no adult was ready to help you in difficult situations, that feeling planted the seed of low self-esteem. Clearly, it was *not* okay that you didn't get tucked into bed, that your birthdays always ended in chaos, that your mother drank herself into a stupor every Christmas Eve rather than celebrating the holiday with you. The problem is, if there was no third party around to witness your situation and say or do something about it, you had no way of knowing that it was abnormal, unacceptable behavior on your parents' part.

Nearly all people raised in a home shaped by addiction have problems with self-worth. You aren't alone. *You are lovable! You are interesting! You are strong!* And poor self-esteem is not a part of your personality but rather a problem you are willing and able to tackle. The task now falls to you to do the work. While you may feel weak and insecure, in reality, you have massive inner strength that is important to recognize and associate yourself with. As the child of someone with an addiction, you have emerged from one of the most devastating upbringing conditions that can afflict a family.

To be realistic, it is unlikely that *all* the news from your past is bad. You couldn't have survived childhood and adolescence in a family with substance abuse problems and made it to adult life without having some resources to draw upon. True, you may not have had supportive parents, but there may have been other positive influences—a grandmother who pampered you and welcomed your visits or someone else who nurtured your development in some way. You may have had a sort of second home with the family of a close friend. Any such relationships can be resources for you to draw on as you revisit your history. Take stock of any such resources you had, as well as those you have now.

Perhaps you've never thought of yourself as a strong and resourceful human being, but you are. Going into therapy or reading a book like this is not a sign of defeat but an indication that you are sincerely trying to find your core and get in touch with your strength. In a way, that process can actually be refreshing since it distracts you from constantly thinking about what others expect of you and hoping you meet those expectations.

Self-Esteem and Self-Confidence

Self-esteem is about your right to *be*, the intrinsic value of your own company, and your own existence. What value do you have in just being who you are without doing something in order for someone to like you? To what degree do you feel you have the same rights as other people?

Self-confidence, by comparison, is confidence in your own *abilities* and in knowing that you are good at something, that there is something you have mastered. Although someone raised in a home shaped by alcohol abuse is likely to have low self-esteem, she might also have varying degrees of confidence. One person might know that he or she is good at certain tasks or kinds of work, while someone else's low self-confidence might jumble the picture, skewing her assessment of her own performance in one direction or another. And a sense of confidence can wax and wane and even swing wildly, changing from high at one moment to low at the next.

Your degree of self-esteem is what is expressed when you are not playing a role, when you step up for yourself or reach out to meet people—for example, when you visit your in-laws for the first time or are introduced to new friends, or get into a situation in which other people know each other, but no one knows you. Such circumstances will let you know whether your self-esteem is high or low. If you feel as if you have no significance and don't have the same status as the people around you, those are signs of low self-esteem. Your background lacked the sorts of positive experiences and feedback that would have given you a higher regard for yourself. You never internalized the idea that your presence and contribution to what goes on around you could be of value.

Unwritten Rules

When low self-esteem is part of one's life, shame is too. Do you consider yourself to be as valuable as anyone else, and do you feel relaxed in the company of friends? Do you know how to settle in, say what you want, and feel that what you say is just as important as what someone else says? Or are you self-defeating, always trying to adapt rather than participate?

If you never learned what the norms for interaction are, you may find it hard to state your opinions and dare to be yourself. You may crave recognition, but you have a hard time taking it to heart when you are praised. Receiving praise is not consistent with the image you have of yourself, so you may not understand or trust why someone would give it.

This may be due to embarrassment, but it could also be because you cannot truly see your own value. The result may be that you find it difficult to be in the spotlight, so you sometimes get over apologetic or do silly things to divert attention from yourself. You might say yes more often than no and cover up your feelings if other people upset or injure you. You may get the idea that people really only like you because they don't know you.

Keep this in mind: The emotions you suppress because of low self-esteem, combined with all the inner needs that go unmet, will only stunt your self-esteem further. The exercises in this book are specifically designed to help you feel and acknowledge your emotions in order to help you build your self-esteem and meet your own inner needs.

"I am a child of an alcoholic. If you had met me a couple of years ago, that sentence would have been almost impossible for me to write. Fortunately, today it is not. Just a year ago, I chose to stop seeing my father since I couldn't stand his abuse anymore. I still don't have any contact with him, and that's how it has to be."—Lina

Interactions with Others

High or low self-esteem influences how you are treated. Someone raised in an environment influenced by an addiction can have a hard time listening to their gut feelings when choosing acquaintances and friends. Unable to sort out bad friends from good ones, they risk being poorly treated—being abused, bullied, and in general exposed to unpleasant, even potentially traumatic situations. That habit of making bad choices often carries all the way into adulthood.

Adults and children with high self-esteem will not put up with being treated poorly. But for you, if your self-esteem is low, it can be hard to sort good behavior from bad, and your tolerance for poor treatment can be high. Maybe you've always seen yourself as someone who *attracts* all those bad romantic partners (who may be addicts themselves) or friends who take advantage of you. However, the reality is not that you attract those types of people but that you do not weed them out from your personal circle. You give in to familiarity—keeping yourself open to contact with people whose harshness will remind you of the atmosphere in the home you grew up in. This helps keep your self-esteem low.

Relationships on Hold

Choosing a partner when your mindset is one of low self-worth can ensnare you in a vicious downward spiral: You choose somebody who proves to be unkind to you / You blame yourself and buy into your partner's view of you / You end up unable to stop condemning yourself and construct a positive self-image.

Maybe your friends don't like your choice of partner. Maybe he speaks to you with contempt or cheats on you, is sometimes cruel, even completely disappears at times. Nonetheless, you're reluctant to break it off because, somehow, it "feels right." It's not happy, but it's what you know. It matches the definition of a "loving relationship" that you learned at home while growing up.

Maybe your friendships are usually at a superficial level, or maybe you can only tolerate having one close friend. Having to manage two or three close friends may be too much.

Your low self-regard can even interfere with a relationship with a *good* partner. What if, due to your poor opinion of yourself, you find it difficult to believe that your partner could actually love you you find it difficult to believe that your partner could actually love you due to your poor opinion of yourself? What if you are so skeptical that you require an excessive amount of proof, so much that it puts a strain on the relationship?

Someone who is used to always adapting and never speaking up for herself is likely to find a partner who wants to run the show, who will work on the assumption that your primary concern will always be fitting in with his vision.

Thoughts Are Just Thoughts

Unfortunately, it will take more than good friends and kind partners to convince you that you are wise, sweet, and worthy. Sure, people can say kind words, but it's the critical voice inside your own head that ultimately defines what you believe. The most authoritative voice, as far as you're concerned, is always going to be your own thoughts.

But thoughts are just thoughts. And while they do create your reality, they are not the *truth*. You have power over them—even if you haven't claimed that power just yet.

Your feelings derive from your thoughts. Try to think back to the last time you were uncomfortable or anxious and recall what you thought just before you had that unpleasant feeling. Perhaps you had a bad experience immediately prior, or something made you think that no one liked you, or that you stupidly messed something up. If you didn't get the chance to fully develop as you grew up, you might still be at the mercy of a child's logic and a child's conclusions. Ideas and decisions that made sense at the time but have long since gone obsolete are controlling you because you haven't fully examined them yet. You've built a limited life out of a set of limited, childish ideas. Your job now is to face down those ideas, to say a resounding NO to all the automatic negative and judgmental thoughts you have about yourself.

It is possible to change your perception of yourself, and enrolling in therapy or picking up a book like this is symbolic of the faith you have in that possibility. The world may be the same when you emerge from this work, but your way of being in the world will be different. The energy you may have expended over decades on the notion of changing or rescuing your parents or other people will be yours to channel in a direction that will nourish you and make you happy. After a lifetime of neglect and pain, you deserve that change.

Trapped in Your Own Logic and Mind

Maybe you have fretted excessively over whether you helped enough at work or at home, or whether you attended to everything that needed doing (the dishes, the laundry). Finding things you failed to take care of, you were quick to blame your own selfishness, endlessly racking your brain to figure out what you might have done differently and better.

This constant examining of your performance in an ongoing effort to solve problems can work against you; too much of it can blur your sense of where your responsibilities begin and end, of the dividing lines between your responsibilities and others'. It locks you up in your own solitary space rather than encouraging cooperation, collaboration, and openness with others.

Goodbye to Life in the Background

The effects of building up your self-esteem will not be a secret. Your body will become more lively and expressive, your eyes brighter. You will feel the energy in your cells and see the animation of your face in the mirror. To refer back to the metaphor of a house, there will be more light and life in every room.

Other people will get a clearer sense of who you are because you will feel safe in emerging from behind the facade that you've cowered behind all these years. You will take the initiative more often and take far more risks, saying, *Here I am,* and *This is what I think*. You will dare to *be* in the world and occupy the space around you. Your lovely, unique nature will come into its own as you guide your own life more and more.

Living in the background will no longer be enough, and you'll want to do something about it. Your longing to say no without always feeling that you are a disappointment will seem achievable, and the difference between what your peers get out of life and what you get out of life will start to shrink. You'll begin to get a clearer picture of what you've been missing all this time, and you'll no longer have the patience to make that pointless sacrifice again.

The poison arrows have lodged in your system long enough. It is time to get them out.

EXERCISES: BUILD YOUR SELF-ESTEEM

1. Rate Your Self-Esteem

How would you describe your self-esteem today on a scale of 1 to 10, with one being the lowest and ten the highest? Try to put into words why you rate it at that level. What people and recent situations may have affected that score?

As you start working consciously to strengthen your self-esteem, try keeping track of its ups and downs on a scale like this, and make an effort to understand what affects its level. The more conscious you become of the most influential factors, the better you will cope with destructive habits that eat away at your self-esteem, and the better you will get at creating positive experiences that contribute to creating an image of yourself as valuable, unique, and lovable.

Low self-esteem is maintained by thinking negatively about yourself. Growing up in a home with alcohol problems, you have surely experienced events and circumstances that contributed to creating a falsely negative picture of yourself. If you put yourself in a degraded light with thoughts like "No one likes me" or "If they find out who I really am, they'll leave," you'll send a message to people that they shouldn't have any higher expectations of you than you have of yourself. You may pull away from people because you are convinced that separation is inevitable anyway or try to preempt any praise or recognition they give you, not allowing it to be incorporated into your self-image. If you think about it, you can probably recall occasions when you've done exactly that.

But now you must do the opposite. When you see that people around you are sincere in their praise and/or recognition of you, let it stick! Absorb it and let it nourish you. Self-esteem training is about getting rid of the old distorted picture of yourself once and for all. That image is not you. *It never has been, and it has never been accurate. With an investment of time and patience, you can let it go.*

2. Five Negative Thoughts

Try to zero in on the specifics of your self-image by writing down five negative thoughts you typically have about yourself. Now read over what you've just written. Can you see how it can have a toxic effect on you to think and talk this way? You would never speak like that to someone you admire or love, and yet you are talking like that to yourself. That needs to stop now. Negative thoughts about yourself instantly trigger feelings of discomfort, anxiety, and tension. Developing healthy self-esteem cannot happen as long as you think of yourself as some kind of different, strange, maybe even inhuman person. Whatever sparked those ideas in the first place, they do not paint an accurate picture of you.

Decide that, starting now, you will be kind to yourself and stop thinking such negative things about yourself. You don't deserve it, and you never did. Instead, practice being your own best friend.

3. Five Positive Qualities

Although you may have spent much of your life preoccupied with anxiety and unpleasant experiences, you have also developed many skills and qualities that are beautiful and positive. Make a list of the five qualities you value the most in yourself: You are good at listening to others, for example, or you are a good friend or a good parent to your children. Later in the book, we will focus on working with those important and deeply meaningful values.

As you unhurriedly fill out this list, make sure you are sincere about things that appeal to you. Now is not the time to succumb to someone else's standards or be pestered by the critical voices of your mother or father running through your mind. This is about your inner eye. Who are you, and what do you care about most?

Obviously, you will need to go into this matter more deeply than just filling out this list, but it is an excellent early step toward correcting a distorted self-image.

4. Smiley Faces

For each of the qualities you name, add some kind of indicator of how much you think you use it in your daily life—a smiley face next to each one you use daily, for example, and maybe one that's a little less smiley next to ones you use only infrequently. As you might guess, a sad face belongs next to any good quality you know you have but rarely use, and those are the ones that need your most urgent attention. Begin a campaign to embrace those traits and use them daily.

Building self-esteem requires a combination of thought and behavior. If you have written down that you are a social person, but you do not make time to be with the people you care for, then you're only paying lip service to your desire to improve your self-image. Invite some friends over, call your best friend—make contact!

5. Begin to Cultivate Positive Thoughts About Yourself

The following list of words offers examples of the unique qualities/attributes that we humans perceive as appealing. Select the five that you identify with the most.

Beautiful lovely wonderful **desirable** irreplaceable funny fantastic warm **exciting** interesting imaginative responsible mature inclusive accommodating reliable **real** cheerful positive committed strong reasonable smart humorous **intelligent** kind embracing trustworthy observant loving friendly **magnificent** vigorous **charming steadfast** stable good engaging authentic generous charismatic loyal attractive

accommodating generous **clever** wise brave
patient reliable determined dynamic
sweet sensitive unique clear thorough dedicated
serious handsome competent conscious inventive **creative**
sensual focused playful lively expressive
musical kind **sociable** social convivial
happy open confident giving dutiful
hearty interested present **loving**
fun efficient healthy pretty **understanding** decent
loyal empathic assertive fair **curious**
effective prepared **honest** talented cheerful
alert **fast** particular popular likable natural
enthusiastic resilient **adventurous** innovative loving
entertaining humble self-aware cool
brilliant imaginative engaging ingenious **supportive**
caring **compassionate** well-groomed pleasant
knowledgeable **experienced** forgiving spirited
successful winning creative lucky **steadfast**
tolerant **persistent** skillful fair compelling multi-faceted
professional **worthy** irresistible appreciative
rich remarkable meaningful well-behaved
special valuable **liberated** straightforward strong-willed

Over a period of time, regularly repeat to yourself those five qualities. Say "I am...and I am...," and so on. It's important to begin to see yourself as the person you are! Speak these characteristics out loud as you look at yourself in the mirror and think about them often. If you keep a journal, write them in there, or write them on a piece of paper and tack it somewhere where you'll see them every day.

It is a good idea to keep directing your attention to these qualities every day for a long period. It's like steadily adding, dollar by dollar, to a bank account. Try stretching out the exercise by making a list that pertains to someone else, someone you love and admire. It is often easier to see other's good qualities than our own, but in fact, the good qualities we see in others are sometimes the very ones we share with them!

6. Hold on to Success and Happy Moments

Write down some good qualities or positive, significant experiences that are associated with your biological family. Both small and big things apply. For example, you may think your mother or father was good at traveling with you when you were younger, or you remember your mother growing a vegetable garden and making healthy meals. Perhaps you and other family members had some delightful experiences in nature, or at one time, your parents were very sociable. If you can't recall any good experiences from childhood, choose experiences from your adult life. Creating higher self-esteem is about being closely connected with your positive experiences.

7. Gratitude List

One way to work with maintaining a positive focus in your life is to create a gratitude list in your journal or a notebook to work with every evening before you go to bed. Write down at least ten things you are thankful for, including things that might seem inconsequential. This can be a challenging exercise in the beginning but training your mind to focus on the positive gives you energy. There is always something that is going well, even if you don't notice it.

8. Self-Worth Book

Compile a book just for yourself that contains only materials and words that strengthen your self-worth. Buy an empty notebook whose look suits you. Make sure it has enough room to include pictures. Fill it with photos, clippings, writings. The book can be full of your positive thoughts and dreams for the future.

Your self-worth book will take some time to complete, but you may enjoy it enough that you make a whole series of them. A longer, more sustained project will let you immerse yourself in yourself in a positive way. The result will be a document that reflects more sides of you than you might expect. Think about making something that touches you and that makes you happy when you look at it.

Some possible contents:

- *Photos of people you love, of happy experiences with friends and family. Write short comments to accompany each image.*
- *Photos of yourself in situations that make you smile or about which you feel happy and/or proud. Choose pictures you think are good and that you look good in.*
- *Pictures of your heroes. Maybe there are movie stars, authors, philosophers, religious figures, etc. Write down what you especially admire each one for.*
- *Slogans and quotations that have a lot of meaning for you. This could include your list of strengths and positive attributes as well!*
- *Positive words about yourself. You might include your list from the earlier exercise, or you can make a new one.*
- *Journal-type entries about experiences you want to*

remember. Self-worth strengthens when you hold on to the good experiences that you were part of.
- Writings about things you are thankful for, things you are glad you experienced.
- A text message that made you happy or an email that had meaning for you.
- A list of goals and wishes. (This is also an exercise that will come later in the book, but you can begin working on it now.) Your wishes can be fantastic and ambitious but make the goals you set for yourself realistic and concrete. It's important for people from alcoholic families to make solid plans for the future, to give them a firm horizon to look to.

The process of creating your self-worth book will itself generate a lot of love, joy, and good inner feelings—enjoy it! You can take the book anywhere, even keep it with you all the time. Or you can take it with you when you are on vacation and continue to add items to your different lists—leaf through it as needed to provide yourself with mirror images of all your good sides.

Soon, you will begin to recognize that there is so much more to you than you thought. When that happens, a boost in your self-esteem can't be far behind.

Once you have worked on all these exercises for a couple of months, go back to what you wrote back at the beginning. You will find that you already feel differently.

In connection with these exercises, you might take inspiration from two of Louise L. Hay's books: I Can Do It: How to Use Affirmations to Change Your Life, and You Can Heal Your Life.

EXERCISE: WRITE YOUR LIFE STORY

Childhood, Part 3

Let the questions below guide you as you write the next part of your life story.

What are the best and happiest experiences you remember?

What is the worst situation you experienced as a child?

What were your relationships with your siblings like?

How was school for you? Were your parents involved in your education?

What friends did you have?

What did you find fun and exciting to do as a child?

7

LETTING GO OF TRAUMA AND GROUNDING YOURSELF IN YOUR BODY

All people carry baggage from traumatic experiences, but those who grew up in homes shaped by addiction are especially burdened. It doesn't take a traffic accident or a major disaster to induce trauma.

Saying you have had a traumatic experience means you have lived through an overwhelming situation, but the way you observe a situation determines whether or not it will be traumatic for you. This means that an experience can traumatize you but not necessarily your sister, your friend, or your partner.

There can be trauma in a fall from a bike or from being taken away from your parents. Whatever the event, when you are unable to defend yourself, or there is a breakdown in the inner mechanisms that would otherwise allow you to take action, and you experience strong anxiety from not being able to extract yourself from the situation, the experience is necessarily traumatic. Its adverse effects will follow you unless you do something about it.

"My mother always fell asleep on the couch in the evening. I remember one night when she was sleeping, and I tried to wake her but couldn't. I was very scared because I thought she was dead. I ran down to the basement, where my father often spent evenings when she had passed out. I screamed, "Mom is dead! Mom is dead!" He came up and showed me how to make sure she was breathing. That day I learned how to tell whether she was alive."—Charlotte

Growing up in a family in the context of alcohol abuse can be filled with traumatic experiences. You may have fallen off the jungle gym and taken a hard hit to the head or tripped on the sidewalk and skinned your knee, but your parents didn't seem to take it seriously. Or you received too little support in the course of a painful loss like your parents' divorce or the death of a grandparent. Even just being stranded in your room for hours, alone and sad, without anyone coming to comfort you could imprint you with trauma that will linger in your life.

It is not the specific situation that creates the trauma; it is the experience of it. If you are able to fight or flee, you may not incur any scars, but if you freeze in the situation, helpless, the experience can stay with you. If your parents fought in front of you and your siblings, the child who put herself between the mother and father might have escaped without any trauma because she was able to act. But for the little brother or sister who could only stand by and witness the fight, the damage could be extreme.

The Body's Emergency Alarm System

"Freezing" is sometimes a way to survive, an instinctual mechanism for dealing with a threat. But the forced inaction of freezing can leave a vivid memory of the incident lodged in the body. To function in a healthy way, the body must be allowed to physically do something, say, to turn the wheel of a car to avoid an accident. It must somehow protect itself; the body needs to be allowed to *work through the protective action*. Only when your body gets the chance to complete, in one way or another, a full reaction to a threat, instilling the idea that you can take care of yourself, can you stop carrying the trauma around.

"The weekends were the worst. Dad got drunk first thing in the morning—after all, he had a whole day without the demands of a grueling job, so he could let go. More or less, my mother tried to keep up with him, drinking red wine and beer. Soon, she was drunk, too, 'for fun.' They would be in our sauna, where they often stayed too long because their sense of time was blurred. Dinner was with parents who were having that kind of 'fun.'"—Mona

Traumas that are not worked through can be very persistent, creating a lot of conflict and unrest in your closest relationships. If you experienced being ignored as a child, some event or situation that hints even vaguely at that sort of deprivation might trigger significant anger inside you. You may interpret some small slight as if it were as significant as the original childhood situation. Before you know it, you sense the emotions surging as violently as if you were only a child with your mother or father standing in front of you. Their failure to protect and care for you has reverberated within you down through the years, and even though the trigger in this moment was something your partner or a friend did or said, the real target of your anger is your parents.

Imagine you run across a drunk on the street. The sound of his slurred speech fills you with discomfort and disgust, even makes you physically ill. Like a time machine, the experience takes you back to your childhood, where you recall your parents behaving in the same way. Unfortunately, life presents many undesirable situations that are impossible to avoid, so it is critical that you look your trauma in the eye and begin working on it directly, rather than brainstorming on ways to escape it.

If you often feel uncomfortable in conversations with authority figures—your boss or your child's teacher or even your in-laws, for example—but you don't know why, there is a good chance that turning back the clock will bring you to some sort of trauma that's at the root of your problem. Perhaps you were harshly and unfairly scolded by a parent who drank, and these conversations resurrect a fear of being harshly judged or interrogated. Maybe you never learned that you could be good at something, and you feel as if you're always at a disadvantage. A person who got the idea as a child that elders and the people in charge could not be trusted may have trouble in general with authority figures as an adult.

The pain associated with those circumstances can continue to imprint itself on your personal interactions many years later. Any kind of corrective feedback or criticism from others can feel unbearable, even if you have the good sense to know that it does not mean you are an unworthy person. You may suddenly feel threatened. The feeling that at any minute, everyone will discover how incapable you are, and you will be exposed starts your thoughts and your pulse racing; you may even have heart palpitations. That's what happens when your trauma is allowed to run the show, unidentified and unexamined.

Trauma has a way of locking in a lot of mistaken ideas and distorted images that, if they're not addressed, end up dictating the terms of your identity as an adult, even though they don't present any kind of accurate picture of you.

Trauma caused by violent events can easily be reactivated by incidents that involve no violence. Yes, if your father hit you, then being hit by someone again could bring it all rushing back, but so could being spoken to condescendingly or dismissively if the situation reminds you of how your dad's behavior made you feel. If you were a helpless witness to your father hitting your mother, the sight of someone being treated unfairly, being bullied or verbally attacked, may trigger an outsize surge of anger in you —the two episodes of cruelty and betrayal may seem like much the same thing.

There may be traumatic episodes you don't even remember because they were so upsetting that you needed to distance yourself from them in order to survive. A situation reminiscent of the original experience may reactivate that pain. The unpredictability of those reactions can complicate your relationships with other people; you may feel that the rug is too easily pulled out from under you and that it is hard to trust and believe others. Relationships consequently require a great deal of energy, maybe too much.

Your constant vigilance against the unreliability of others can cost you in terms of openness, honesty, and spontaneity. In the long run, your fear of finding yourself triggered into a seemingly helpless and "frozen" state may lead you to avoid close relationships altogether.

Allow Your Body to Become Your Friend

Triggering episodes don't happen only inside your head. There can also be a powerful physical component as the body seeks to avoid or escape the perceived threat. In the case of extremely violent trauma, it can even reach an extreme called *dissociation*, in which you feel as if you are not present in your own body, or you are in some kind of trance, or someone is right behind you or looking at you. In terms of relationships, this can mean you suddenly aren't fully *present* with the other person; you're unfocused.

Recognizing these unpleasant sensations as the product of traumatic experiences and developing your conscious awareness of those trouble spots is essential to releasing trauma's grip on your life.

Take an inventory of your bodily sensations. Do you tend to take shallow breaths rather than breathing deep into your abdomen? Do you carry a lot of tension or discomfort in your muscles or have a lot of physical ailments that recur or don't seem to go away? Do you think of yourself as being more in your head than in your body? Do you channel your focus away from your body by bathing, dressing, or even swallowing quickly and unconsciously? Are there ways in which you feel ashamed of your body?

Check-in with what is happening in your stomach right now, how you feel as you read this. Are you worried or nervous about something? Do you have an upset stomach? Sometimes, a jumble of thoughts and feelings in your mind is mirrored in a mixed-up, churning assortment of bodily sensations.

If trauma of various kinds was a reality in your childhood, a course of therapy with a psychologist specializing in trauma might be a very good idea, alongside the work you are doing with this book. Various kinds of trauma stem from disconnections in your relationships with other people, circumstances that may have left you lonely and isolated. Sitting with someone who is trained to help you pinpoint those problems and work on them, someone ready to assure you that what happened in your childhood was not okay and acknowledge the trouble it has caused you, can do a great deal of good.

The help of someone trustworthy can be crucial to healing: *A trauma that was created in a relationship must also be healed in a relationship, one that is healthy and strong enough to create new experiences without re-creating the trauma.*

Feel Your Body

All the exercises at the end of this chapter are intended to strengthen your relationship with yourself and your innate ability to self-regulate. They derive from trauma treatment and are evidenced-based to help from the moment you begin applying them. Some are about soothing yourself; others are about building up and nourishing yourself. Others help you sharpen your awareness of your boundaries and your natural right to protect and defend yourself.

Trauma springs from the loss of contact with yourself and your body, so as you work consciously to be more present in your body and aware of your feelings and sensations, you can expect the effects of trauma to lessen. People are sometimes afraid to start this work out of fear that revisiting traumatic experiences will overwhelm them or make them feel threatened. But most of the exercises in this chapter were developed by the psychologist Peter Levine, whose method does not center on reliving the horror of trauma. After all, reliving the worst elements of trauma runs a risk of generating even more of it, and that is not the point: The point is to *free* yourself from trauma, not to relive it.

A Note on the Exercises

The process of delving into a troublesome past is different for everyone. If you get scared along the way and do not feel like you can manage your reactions, give yourself credit for recognizing that and put the brakes on the process until you are in a safe situation with, for example, a therapist. Specifically, if you feel intense fear or panic, stop the exercise. All other feelings, even intense ones, are allowable and won't harm you. Do not be afraid of the tears that may come with getting in touch with your grief—the crying will eventually stop.

This kind of work will call on both your internal and external resources. External resources include people you have close ties with and places where you can go for help and support, etc. Internal ones include personal traits, such as your sense of humor, your patience, or your ability to manage uncomfortable feelings while maintaining a belief in positive outcomes.

When you work with your inner resources, it is perfectly natural for sadness, anxiety, or anger to crop up. In fact, those are generally signs that your deep-rooted problems are beginning to relax their grip on your subconscious. This is a good thing, so don't be afraid—some of these feelings may be old ones that never got enough of a chance to express themselves earlier in your life.

The fact that you may still have a mother or father who drinks can be saddening, extremely stressful, almost impossible to accept. When you permit yourself to feel the emotions that come with this work, you acknowledge the loss you have suffered and may still have to live with. Anger and disappointment are part of it, and so is a certain amount of anxiety. Getting in contact with these emotions is an essential part of the process and an indicator that your healing process is well underway. Be gentle and patient with yourself as you work through the exercises. Allow the process to guide you into the real contact that you have longed to have with yourself.

EXERCISES: MAKE FRIENDS WITH YOUR BODY

(All exercises in this chapter, except as noted, are inspired by Peter A. Levine's Healing Trauma: A Pioneering Program for Restoring the Wisdom of Your Body.*)*

1. Grounding

Sit in a chair in a confident, upright posture. Put your hands on your thighs or the lower part of your stomach. Place your feet firmly on the floor, hip-width apart, and feel your connection to the floor through the soles of your feet. It is up to you whether to close your eyes or just maintain a soft focus in front of you without looking at anything specific.

Notice whether you can feel energy anywhere in your body: your legs or arms, feet, or hands. You may feel it as a quivering or tingling, or a kind of heat, or some other sort of motion flowing freely inside you. Sit still and pay attention to what you are feeling right *now. No matter what your experiences are, be in this moment, focusing on what is there now.*

This simple exercise will feel different to you every day. On some days, you may experience differences between the right and the left sides of your body, and at other times you'll mostly feel the upper part of your body or your legs and feet. Be aware of these differences.

A grounding exercise like this is absolutely essential for regulating your nervous system. From the first time you do it, it will help you relax your body by reestablishing your connection to the earth beneath your feet.

Trauma causes many people to lose their grounding, leaving their body out of balance and lacking a confident center of grav-

ity; you may experience that as if you were floating or flying around and not fully present in your body. It is important to reestablish your grounding. We experience feelings in our body, and when you develop good grounding, you give yourself a solid foundation from which to repair trauma and reconcile with past experiences.

Working daily with this little exercise, you will experience more peace and power within two to four weeks. Most adult children of alcoholics will benefit tremendously from it. And the sense of security it creates will serve as a good launching pad for the next exercises in the book. Allow yourself the time to complete the exercise every day, at least once a day, for at least two weeks.

2. Be Present in Your Body

This exercise is designed to regulate tension and unpleasant emotions.

Assume the same seated position as in the grounding exercise. Raise one foot a short distance off the floor, and bend and wiggle it back and forth and around, to loosen up your ankle. Repeat with the other foot. Take care to do it slowly and be aware of each of your movements.

Next, loosen one knee joint by bending and stretching. Bend and stretch several more times before changing legs. Then sit still and feel the energy flowing through your legs.

With one arm at a time, circle and bend your wrists, then your elbows, then finally your shoulders, letting the motion loosen your shoulder joints. Sit still a moment and be aware of the energy in your hands, arms, and shoulders.

Look over one shoulder and turn your head slowly from one shoulder to the other while allowing your eyes to look at the things around you.

Sit quietly and sense what is happening throughout your body.

The exercise is designed to free up the energy in your legs and arms, shoulders, and neck. It releases tension and blocked energy (energy often gets blocked in the joints). Pay attention to the differences between before you do the exercise and after. When your energy is not blocked, you will feel a greater lightness and closer contact with yourself. The exercise can be useful in stressful situations in which you find yourself especially nervous and tense. It also makes a good preparation for, say, meeting with others or tackling a thorny problem. It takes just five or 10 minutes.

3. Inner and Outer Resources

Draw a line on a piece of paper to divide it into two. Make a heading on each half: "Inner Resources" on the left side and "Outer Resources" on the right side. Then begin to fill in the two columns.

Inner resources are those qualities and values and other intangible things that strengthen you and that you can thank for many of the good things in your life: courage, love, joy, imagination, humor, intelligence, kindness, pleasant memories, etc. "Outer resources" are the inner ones' counterparts out in the world: friends, a good therapist, your partner, listening to music, candlelight, being out in nature, swimming, visiting beautiful places, being with animals, exercise, etc.

This exercise aims to heighten your awareness of the resources you can draw on when facing challenges or simply when you desire a greater connection with your body. There is strength in this kind of enhanced awareness, and it can change your experience of yourself in the world.

If you find it difficult to believe that you are strong and lovable and interesting, then it is very important that the two lists that come out of this exercise do not end up in a drawer somewhere, ignored. Take a look at them every day; that investment of only a minute or two of your time just might change your way of seeing yourself and your life.

4. Good-Energy Booster Visualization

Begin with the grounding exercise to establish contact with your breath and with the solidity of your feet on the ground, and to become centered. Then, sitting with your eyes closed, think of a happy moment in your life. Listen to your body as you do this, and notice where you feel changes. Focus on the specific feelings that this happy memory gives you.

Now, assign your favorite color to that emotion. Picture that color spreading throughout your body, infusing each cell. Remain seated for five to seven minutes, allowing yourself to luxuriate in the happiness that permeates you.

This exercise helps you hold on to good experiences and connect with them. It is also useful in building inner resources that can help you release old betrayals, feelings of sadness, and traumatic experiences. Doing this exercise every day for an extended period of time can help people of all ages from alcoholic homes who tend to worry and be preoccupied with negative thoughts.

[This exercise was inspired by Irene Henriette Oestrich's book Selvværd og nye færdigheder – manual til dig i udvikling *[Self-worth and new capabilities: A handbook for your development].*

5. Pet Exercise

If you have a pet (a dog or cat or horse is probably best for this exercise), you can draw strength from that relationship in ways that can make you feel more present, grounded, and in touch with your body.

Put your hands on the animal's body and, if possible, your head on its chest. Listen to its breathing and heartbeat. Animals are completely, naturally present, and by being with them, you can let their natural rhythm regulate and settle you. Join the animal in being present right now. Just minutes of this can be useful.

Coexisting with animals grounds us, and it is no coincidence that many adult children of alcoholics have sought and found comfort all their lives in attachment to animals. Tuning in to an animal's nervous system has a regulatory effect on humans, and animals are positive, stabilizing company. This exercise may open you even more to your love for your pet and expand your sense of how important your interactions are for your well-being.

6. Physical Exercise

Working out is good for you. It strengthens you and releases endorphins that elevate your mood. It also loosens up your joints, where energy might bog down. Regular exercise can be a source of balance, power, and courage when you are working to release abuse patterns from your past.

What sort of exercise? Any kind! Walking is a form of exercise. Yoga, Tibetan Five Rites, qigong, running, swimming, calisthenics, climbing, cycling, dance—any one or combination of those will work as a perfect supplement to this book. Saunas in tandem with ice-cold baths, showers, or cold-water swimming will also give your mood a boost.

7. *A Mindful Shower*

This is a gentle exercise in which you shower from top to toe. Hot water calms your nerves and provides a good, safe experience of being present in your body.

Hold a handheld showerhead a few inches from your body. Feel the water on your skin. Try saying something to correspond with every area at which you direct the water: "This is my arm, this is my belly, this is my right foot." Say it in whatever way seems natural to you. You can repeat those statements as you dry yourself off or as you apply body lotion.

The purpose of this exercise is to become more present in your physical self, to observe your various body parts. Take the time to be observant, curious, and caring toward your body.

Many people take their body's cooperation for granted, bathing in a hurry and paying little attention to the sensations of water flowing, of scent, and the skin being warmed. Taking a little more time to shower and dry and possibly moisturize your body with a nice lotion is a form of self-care. Mindfulness is about being present in the moment. Every time you take a bath can be an opportunity to be more aware of yourself in your body in that moment. When you add the further step of speaking to and acknowledging the parts of your body, it situates you more firmly in your physical self, and not just in your head.

8. Push Away

Sit with your feet on the floor. Bend both arms and hold your hands in front of your shoulders as if you were about to push something or someone away from you. Slowly begin the movement of pushing away—it might help to imagine pushing a specific person or thing—until both arms are fully stretched out in front of you. Keep your eyes open but focus on what's happening inside your body as you push. Repeat the exercise five or six times, then sit back and feel whatever is going on in your body. Notice all the sensations: Feel the chair and the floor supporting you, the texture of your clothes. Feel the muscles under your skin, feel your energy, your heart rate, your breath. Feel your entire being.

We are naturally prepared to defend ourselves by using aggression when we are threatened or attacked. But many people who grew up in alcoholic homes have learned to block their own natural aggression, to the point that having their own boundaries violated may even seem normal to them. Sometimes that unacknowledged sense of violation can build up to the point where it detonates in a disproportionate expression of anger. To break down this process, this exercise is aimed at building up your natural and innate ability to defend and protect yourself.

You and only you are entitled to decide how closely you want other people to be in relation to your body. This exercise clarifies your own feelings and trains you to respond and move or push away when something is experienced as a threat.

9. Pendulation

Pendulation *is a term that Peter A. Levine has incorporated into the field of psychology. It comes from mathematics, where it refers to movement occurring between two poles. That image is useful when doing this exercise, which can be helpful if you feel bad or emotionally out of balance. (NOTE: This exercise is very demanding. If you think it is not working or have difficulty focusing on your resources, for example, and are feeling overwhelmed, do not do it. It's not dangerous, but it is unlikely to benefit you if you are experiencing discomfort. In that case, do not be afraid to seek help. Talk to a therapist and wait until you are back in balance before attempting it again.)*

Start with the preliminary grounding exercise from a seated position. Focus on a good feeling and enjoy it. Think of a person you love (it might even be someone who is no longer living, but who has been important to you), a pleasant situation, a loving memory, something good that just happened to you. Select the image and memory you are most drawn to and focus on it.

Allow the image of the situation or person to occupy your mind's eye fully. Be aware of how your body reacts to it and to where, specifically, in your body, you can feel your positive response. Take note of it: This area and feeling are a resource for you. Notice what it's like and how it feels. Perhaps it is like a current of energy that is moving around. Maybe it has a color. Maybe it generates strong feelings such as joy, love, tenderness, gratitude, etc. Take the time to explore this inner space.

Now, let your attention swing to the outer edge of this resource of yours, to where you can sense its edge or boundary. Allow your focus to rest there briefly before returning to the center point for a moment. Then let your attention slowly make its way back to the edge—the meeting place between this pleasure-filled space and areas where discomfort may reside—and when you reach the edge, pause for a moment.

Repeat this pendulum swing between resource and proximity to discomfort about four times. Then end the exercise by going to the center point of the resource and see the image or feel this spot again.

Finally, return to the room. How are you feeling right now? What do you feel in your body? Has something settled, perhaps? Do you sense a little more space inside? Has any of the imbalance and discomfort you felt been reduced or maybe even completely subsided? If so, the exercise has been beneficial.

EXERCISE: WRITE YOUR LIFE STORY

Childhood, Part 4

Let the following questions and prompts guide you as you write the next part of your life story.

Describe the general situation regarding alcohol in your childhood household.

Describe a typical day when your mother or father drank.

In just a few words, how would you describe the way your parents raised you?

Overall, what was it like to be you? What do you think (or what have you been told) it was like to be your various siblings?

8

NEEDS - MET AND UNMET

This pyramid diagram formulated by psychologist Abraham Maslow laid out the hierarchy of needs common to all humans. As the pyramid illustrates, you cannot reach the top level, the level of self-actualization, if an array of basic, foundational needs are not met first. In a healthy family, children work their way up the pyramid. But someone who has grown up in a home impacted by alcohol may have missed out on some of the basics and ended up having to channel as much energy into the lowest, most fundamental steps as the upper ones.

Needs are rarely met in homes where addictions are present, and children are often called on to take care of themselves and the alcoholic parent as well. Trust and sturdiness never develop.

The problem is, a child doesn't really know what he needs, and someone who grows up with unmet needs may well grow into an adult who has difficulty satisfying them for himself. Shame over even having needs is common among people raised in a home shaped by alcohol, but it's obviously built on a false perception: Each and every one of us has needs, needs that must be met for the sake of our well-being.

The absence of safe, open collaboration in the meeting of needs can have a range of negative effects, including the need to cheat to get your needs met or shame for having them in the first place. From these, in turn, can come problems of all sorts, from substance abuse to food/eating disorders to addictive habits like smoking. Some of these try to compensate for an inner emptiness with destructive activities similar to the habits you saw in your parents; to have an addiction is to (re)create a state of neglect.

"It was as if there was always a big part of me that could not feel satisfaction or find peace. On the outside, it was as if the whole thing was okay, but I became self-destructive and often drank away my prospects for success. I sabotaged the situation and everything that had been good."—Brian

Value Your Own Needs

The satisfaction that comes from fulfilling natural needs such as going for a walk, doing homework, or talking with a good friend may not be something you know. This is what's behind the idea "be your own caring parent." You must take over the parent's job of taking care of yourself and no longer subconsciously wait for someone else to come and do it. Adopting this role gives you the opportunity to ask yourself a crucial question: *What do I need?*

When an aspect of your life is not being nourished and enriched, there is a lack, or hunger, that creates tension and stress in the body. How well do you tune into the signals your body sends? Perhaps you aren't aware of them at all.

The needs that are not being met throw a spotlight on the places where you may still not be valuing yourself enough. Perhaps you have a hard time taking responsibility for meeting your needs, perhaps you do not know how, or perhaps you have been letting other people try to do it for you. You'd be amazed at some of the ways these things can manifest themselves. Maybe you don't eat healthy food or don't get enough sleep, or you somehow don't manage to notice when you're hungry. Maybe you don't respond right away to the need to go to the toilet—you just hold it in!

Some needs are physical; others are social. Unmet physical needs can lead to an inability to function well. In contrast, unmet social needs can leave you lonely, for one thing, but also have repercussions in your material, financial life. Many find it difficult to arrange for decent housing, get insurance or various benefits, or even be properly paid for their work. The stress of not being in control of economic conditions further worsens the situation by consuming so much energy.

Maybe there are areas in your life where you don't do enough to safeguard your rights, so you live with uncertainty on some fronts and without adequate care. There may be injustice affecting you that you feel powerless to stand up to. You must begin to have conversations about these things, both with other people and with yourself.

If you are the sort of person thought of as a people pleaser, recognize that consideration for yourself counts far more than the consideration you give your bank manager, your boss, or your parents. You do not always need to put yourself last, and you do not need to please people at the expense of living in decent circumstances. At the same time, someone who is just the opposite, overly aggressive, may end up sabotaging the fulfillment of her needs. Both extremes tend to generate poor-quality personal connections, but your life does not have to reflect either of them.

While the needs on Maslow's pyramid are generally universal, how you deal with them is also determined by the personality you were born with. Many will find contentment in taking care of the most basic needs and not pursuing some great self-actualization; having an herb garden or being a hobby painter is enough, without scrambling for experiences at the apex of the pyramid. Others will be more driven. Wherever you are on the scale, when your needs are met, you are in balance and in flow.

EXERCISES: FULFILL YOUR NEEDS

These exercises are about looking at the variety of your needs.

1. The Hierarchy of Needs

Using Maslow's pyramid as a model, write down how you relate to your different needs. Draw a circle around those needs that you are already aware of. Take credit for them. It is important for your development to see and recognize what you are doing and what works for you.

Do you have particular problems with taking care of some of your needs? If yes, write down which ones cause you problems. If you can, describe the reasons why. What is your relationship with food, for example? And what was it as a child? Are you careful to eat regularly and healthy? Do you only eat because you have to, swallowing the food just so the feeling of being hungry will stop? Or do you savor and enjoy your food?

Think back on your childhood regarding this subject. Describe how eating was in your family. How were your meals? Did you eat together? Did you eat breakfast? Did you get lunch at school? Did you eat dinner? What did you eat? What did you like or not like to eat? What lines can you draw between the treatment of and attitude toward food in your childhood home and the way you eat now?

No matter which needs you think need addressing, try to ask yourself clarifying questions like those. Meanwhile, the needs you have not circled are potential areas for you to work on next.

If you have needs at the very bottom—on the basic physical level—of Maslow's hierarchy, it will be beneficial to begin cultivating more compassion here before moving further up and through the pyramid to the other unmet needs. For instance, in terms of food, you must learn to listen more carefully to your body's signals by eating when you feel hungry and resting when you feel tired.

Try to be very concrete and make a plan for how you can, daily, cultivate compassion for the physical needs you have problems with. How can you incorporate those measures into your daily routine? When you experience yourself staying in tune with and consistently meeting your physical needs, then choose new needs to address, higher up in the pyramid.

Dealing with some of the needs of the pyramid may require interaction with other people. Meeting these needs is not just a matter of deciding to change—it will take practice and help from others who already have strong skills in areas you may lack. Simply spending time with friends can help develop your social skills, as can therapy.

2. Do You Have an Addiction?

About 25 percent of adult children of alcoholics are at risk of developing an addiction of some kind. There are numerous reasons for this. Some have a genetic propensity toward drug addiction. Others simply haven't had enough exposure to ways of dealing with problems other than their parents' addictive model.

People who were raised in the context of alcohol abuse tend to suffer from stress and neglect, and many are left with psychological wounds whose pain they try to escape by numbing themselves in one way or the other. They may also seek a safety valve for the pressure of having to constantly attend to a parent's needs rather than their own.

People will seek calm and freedom from the pain of unpleasant emotions in a wide range of ways. They might find comfort in sugar or fast food; some might develop eating disorders. Others disappear into the world of the internet and video games, and some become addicted to alcohol. You may resort to yet other ways of escaping the troublesome parts of yourself.

Do you have or have you had problems with abuse of some kind —eating, shopping, drinking, smoking, gambling, relationships, sex? If so, describe them in writing. Describe the situation and share your thoughts about it. Allow yourself to feel the emotions that get stirred up by this exercise. Pain, shame, tension, anxiety —give your feelings space and write them down. Some depen-

dencies attempt to compensate for unmet needs, and once you begin taking care of those needs, the dependencies will go away. Others can turn into genuine addictions that you will need help to cure. **If you are currently struggling with addiction, do not hesitate to seek help immediately.**

3. Nourishment Journal

Over the next week, compile a logbook of everything you ate and when you ate it. Flesh it out with information such as:

- The amount of each item you ate
- A description of how you ate the meal (Fast? Slow? Enjoyed it? Didn't enjoy it?)
- Who you ate with
- Your attitudes toward food and your feelings about it

After a week's worth of entries, you should be able to come to some conclusions about the role of food in your life. If those conclusions don't seem particularly healthy or life-affirming, make an effort to revise your relationship with food.

For example, if you become aware that you have difficulty relaxing and being present around a meal, commit to slowing down and being more in-the-moment when you eat. If you note that you eat very irregularly, try to get more structure into your meals. Start making sure that you have food on hand so you can eat breakfast, lunch, and dinner. And give yourself time to digest comfortably: Finish your last meal three to four hours before going to bed in the evening.

You can change your eating habits to ensure that your basic diet is nourishing and enjoyable. If your diet is made up of a lot of sugar and/or fat, perhaps a lot of fast food, your body may not be *getting the nutrition it needs, and you may often find yourself tired and drained a while after your meals. Cut down on sugar, excess carbohydrates, and fat. Lowering your sugar intake, in particular, may be a little challenging at first, but the craving for it fades quickly.*

For many people, eating in company is fraught with problems. Do you experience shame and/or other sorts of discomfort eating with others? Examine that issue by writing down the thoughts that occur to you about it. What are you ashamed of? Eating is fundamentally about taking care of yourself, and if you don't consider yourself worthy of care, tension may develop inside you. Shame and tension of that kind can be toxic. You need to realize that you deserve care and comfort, which applies to eating and every other area of your life.

4. A Mindful Meal

Make a meal for yourself (and others too, perhaps) that is more than just a meal. Instead of mere sustenance, put something together that is clearly about love and caring. Take the time to prepare something healthy and tasty, and create a comforting, positive setting for it: Light some candles, put on some beautiful music, and set a table that is nicer and more inviting than your usual. Present the food in an appetizing way. If you share this meal with others, make sure they are people you are comfortable with and who are comfortable with you, so nothing will distract you from the caring, pleasant atmosphere you've created.

Eat slowly, and make sure to savor each bite. Take in the tastes, the aromas, the textures, the look of it all. Listen to your feelings and let yourself take pleasure in the entire meal and all its trappings.

Even if there is food left on your plate or your guests continue to eat, stop eating when you feel full or drowsy. Notice how that fullness feels in your stomach. If you have to, close your eyes and focus your whole attention on it. You may be in the habit of letting your eyes control how much you eat, but the eyes often commit us to more food than we can healthily finish. The more attention you pay to those inner signals, the better able you will be to regulate the amount you eat.

Going forward, be more aware of nourishing yourself. Make plenty of time to eat. Be present *as you eat, focusing on the meal itself and not a host of* distractions. *Avoid eating in a noisy and stressful environment. Look for the peace and relaxation to be had from your meal.*

EXERCISE: WRITE YOUR LIFE STORY

Youth, Part 1

Let the questions and prompts below guide you as you write the next part of your life story.

Write about the major events that your family experienced (e.g., divorce, moving, changing schools, etc.)

Who were the important people in your youth?

When did you have your first sexual experience?

What joys did you experience?

What disappointments did you experience?

What did you think was exciting?

9

BE YOUR OWN LOVING PARENT, BECOME YOUR OWN BEST FRIEND

One characteristic of a confident person is that he is comfortable both when alone and in the company of other people. A person who grew up in a family shaped by alcoholism might well be unhappy whether he is alone or with others. Many experience panic when their partner goes out the door or when they face the prospect of spending some days at home alone with no plans. They may end up turning on the TV, turning up the music, making every effort to drown out their own inner voices. Left alone with their own judgmental thoughts, they criticize themselves and ruminate endlessly.

Being alone is something you must master. Simply spending time alone is a healthy and organic form of self-regulation. It is not possible to be with other people constantly and also be aware and present. Being in balance requires some healthy time alone. Think of it as a cycle similar to inhaling and exhaling, waves rolling in and out, or one season following another. These kinds of alternation keep the world in balance, and the same applies to your inner self.

The challenge is to create a positive relationship with yourself and consciously work on being comfortable in your own company. You have to build up confidence in yourself to the point that you *genuinely want to be with yourself.* Self-hatred is a bad platform for self-development, and it is possible to have a loving relationship with yourself instead and come to love yourself. You must decide to want good things for yourself and then take the initiative to create guidelines on how to spend time with yourself.

When you do something for yourself and start to spend quality time with yourself, you give yourself value. You let go of old messages like *I'm not worth anything,* or *I have no significance.* This has a direct, positive effect on your self-esteem.

At some point in your life, you may have developed unpleasant associations with being alone, which might involve being ostracized or feeling ashamed. Maybe you cut yourself off from the rest of the world because you were afraid to let others see the "real" you. That shame over feeling different or alienated from other people may be anchored so deeply that judgmental thoughts and inner criticism plague any time you spend alone.

Being alone may be an ordeal for you because you've never had the chance to glimpse the good things that come from being in a healthy relationship with yourself. You may interpret all focus on yourself as being selfish and self-absorbed and be disinclined to take yourself seriously. But there's nothing egotistical about spending time alone; in fact, it's essential to being a whole person.

You need to see time with yourself as something secure and meaningful rather than harsh isolation imposed upon you. You need to develop a vision of your alone time as a place where you tend to your own needs, develop yourself, and enjoy your own company, and in general, do something pleasant and beneficial.

Do not equate solitude with a fear of some kind of abandonment you experienced as a child—that can taint your relationship with others, putting you on edge in their company because you fear they may leave you. You may take unfair advantage of them by seeking out their company just to avoid being alone. Or you may risk overwork because it helps you avoid being home alone. In general, a fear of being alone may steer you toward various kinds of bad choices.

Independence and Togetherness

Independence and community are closely related. Developing your autonomy and independence involves learning how to maintain a sense of being part of a community even when you are by yourself. You learn to carry the reassuring spirit of others in your mind so that you remain in their company, whether they are physically present or not. An inability to do this can generate loneliness, anxiety, and feelings of abandonment.

"I have gotten better about being caring and tolerant toward myself. When I get anxious and have catastrophic thoughts, I try to calm myself by saying that it's okay; I'm afraid, but it's okay to have that feeling. Trying to be my own caring parent means that I address my feelings rather than fighting against them."—Anna

When You Close the Doors

As you work with this book, begin to insert a little bit of alone time into each day's schedule. Commit to a certain amount of time with yourself every day, in a way that gives you pleasure and security. You'll find that focusing more on being alone actually makes you better at being yourself with other people.

For someone raised in the context of alcohol abuse, a habit of focusing too intently on other people's moods can make it easy to lose one's focus on oneself. You may continuously monitor the people around you's mental and emotional states instead of attending to your own inner state. It may dawn on you, for example, that in the course of a whole weekend with your partner, you invested so much attention in her that you might as well have been absent the entire time—you lost the ability to sense yourself. If this is something that happens to you, it is vital that you consciously get back in touch with yourself.

Go out for a walk or a run or sit down and write how you're feeling in the moment or engage in some simple form of meditation in a private place. The trick is to remove yourself from the company of others when you sense that you're losing track of yourself in that company.

Time spent alone is not about escaping other people. In fact, when you can enjoy your own company and occupy your alone time, you strengthen your ability to interact with others. Think of it as closing the doors for a while now so you can open them even wider when you rejoin the others. Likewise, being alone is not the same as being lonely. Solitude is not a place where you hide from people but rather a home base where you are learning to be yourself. If you are willing to put in the work, you can make that home base someplace welcoming.

EXERCISES: DISCOVER YOUR CONNECTION TO YOURSELF

1. Find Your Inner Safe Place

This is a relaxation exercise.

Sit on a yoga mat or a blanket with your eyes closed. Allow your arms to open slightly to the side and your legs to widen. Instruct your body to begin to relax.

Notice the natural pattern of your breathing, how the air flows in and flows out. Now try to pinpoint a little break between your inhalation and your exhalation. Feel it as a still, quiet moment. Inhaling through your nose, fill your lungs deeply, then linger for just a moment at that still, quiet point before slowly exhaling through your mouth.

Repeat this three times, and then let your breathing fall back into its natural pattern.

There is a safe place somewhere inside you, and you can always find it by simply closing your eyes and breathing calmly. Take the time to find that place. It may seem to occupy a certain location in your body. Perhaps you sense colors there, or energy that feels like bubbles or swirls. Maybe it feels watery or airy. If it's somewhere specific, try placing your hands over that area and connecting with the peace and quiet that reside there.

Now return to the room you're in, open your eyes, and gently stretch to reoccupy your body fully.

Your inner safe place is always accessible to you. Go to it if you feel sad, worried, or angry, or you just need some peace of mind. Close your eyes and follow your breath.

2. Body Scanning

This exercise should take about five minutes.

Sit upright in a chair with your feet hip-width apart. Loosen up your shoulder and neck area by shrugging your shoulders straight upward and dropping them down again. Turn your head gently to one side and then the other.

Take three deep breaths through your nose. Fill your lungs completely and hold your breath for a moment before slowly breathing out through your mouth.

Now let your breath fall back into its natural pattern.

Feel your feet to establish good contact with the earth. This can be calming. Close your eyes, or unfocus your vision and let your gaze rest somewhere in front of you.

Make a mental scan of your body, letting your consciousness sense how it feels right now.

Notice whether you are experiencing pleasant feelings or uncomfortable ones, whether you are relaxed or tense in different parts of your body. Without yielding completely to it, focus your attention on the unpleasant spots. Be curious about them, and try not to judge yourself if you are feeling bad.

There is always a reason when an emotion lodges in your body. Feel it, and if possible, name it. Ask yourself why it is there.

Now leave the unpleasant sensations behind and direct your attention instead to areas of calm, comfort, and pleasure. Once again, feel the firm connection between the earth and your feet, and tie it in your mind to the positive areas.

3. Angel Exercise

Sit in a chair with your back straight and your feet hip-width apart on the floor. Drop your arms to your sides. Imagining that you are a child lying in the snow or on the sand at a beach, take a deep breath, and, as you do, make "angel wings": Lift and stretch your arms so that your hands meet high above your head.

Follow your breathing by lowering your wings as you exhale until they point to the floor once again. Do this five to eight times.

This exercise strengthens your physical sense of the space around you. Many adult children of alcoholics find it hard to set boundaries that determine how close other people can get. The area within the span and sweep of your angel wings is your own personal space, and it is up to you whether to admit anyone into it. Regularly doing this exercise will make your sense of personal space more concrete.

EXERCISE: WRITE YOUR LIFE STORY

Youth, Part 2

Let the questions below guide you as you write the next part of your life story.

How do you describe who you were as a young person?

Looking back, what do you remember feeling inside?

From your current vantage point as an adult, what do you see yourself as having struggled with back then in comparison with the other youngsters you knew?

What kinds of activities did you engage in?

How did your parents' alcohol abuse influence you and your family during your youth?

10

RECOGNIZE THE ROLES YOU PLAY

"My parents are each two different people when they drink and when they're sober. Mom is aggressive and angry when she is drunk and depressed when she is sober. Dad is an open, sensitive, and a man of the world when he's drunk, but a petty, angry, closed person when he's sober. As a child, I never knew just who I was dealing with."—Lene

Certain roles commonly arise in families influenced by alcohol, as children are forced to carry out and compensate for functions that are unfulfilled by the drinking parent. These often correspond to birth order; in a classic framework, the oldest child might become the Hero, the second child, the Scapegoat, the third the Forgotten Child, and the youngest the Clown.

The Hero takes charge of all the practical matters—ensuring, for example, that the siblings get to bed on time and are picked up after school. The Scapegoat shoulders the blame for everything that goes wrong, getting no recognition or reward for her achievements. The Forgotten Child does not require any attention or help and becomes virtually invisible. In contrast, the

Clown supplies comic relief, distracting everyone from their difficulties by saying cute and funny things.

Did you play one of these roles as a child, or something equally archetypal? What kind of role have you gravitated toward as an adult? Is it similar to the one you played as a child? What implications might that role-playing have for your personal relationships and for the way you organize your life today?

Of course, no one is necessarily confined to just one role. You might switch between various roles, depending on the specific context. There may be one for when you're with your partner and another when you're at work. Significant changes in your life, like a new job or a divorce, may prompt a switch. Or maybe the role-playing is not a full-time thing and becomes necessary only in the context of coping with stress.

"I tried to cover up his problem by not inviting friends over. My sister and I never asked him for help or to take us places because we knew he wasn't up to it, especially in the evening. Instead, we asked people for rides, and we biked everywhere we could."
—Mona

Each role comes with its own set of problems as well as its own potential strengths and values, but ultimately you need to distinguish between your role and your real identity, your core self. It is important to remember that the role is not your personality but merely something you adopted to survive. Many of the traits you adopted had nothing to do with you in the first place, and you can let them go.

It may be unnerving to realize that the role is not your identity. After all, that leaves the logical question, *If I'm not that, then who am I?* You must get in touch with yourself to find out, and then you must develop a sense of security in that self. But don't be in a hurry to discard all the qualities of the role; not all of them will be negative. Instead, identify and work with them to maximize the strengths and abilities the role instilled in you.

"I am the daughter of an alcoholic. I am the daughter of a mother who has had cancer twice and a father with a tendency to get blood clots. I am a victim; I am an actor in disguise. And unfortunately, I am one of many. But I am much more than that. I am the only one who has taken a stand against my father and his abuse. I have chosen my own life, and I've fought to get where I am today."—Lina

In Relation to Your Siblings

Your relationships with your siblings are where the remnants of your role-playing can get troublesome. It can be tough to remind yourself that the roles you all assumed were not, in fact, freely chosen and didn't reflect your true identity. Even so, they may have been instrumental in complicating your interactions, and sometimes a sibling will even sever contact over the ramifications of your role-playing.

Conflicts can easily arise based on these inauthentic identities. Even when there is tremendous love and a deep connection, relationships contingent on those obsolete roles can end up unhealthy and enmeshed rather than appropriate in the long run. If, for example, a younger sibling grew up receiving the closeness and care from a heroic older sister or brother that her parents were incapable of giving, her attempts to free herself from the dependency can leave the older Hero sibling feeling betrayed and let down. Suddenly, it's the older one whose identity feels threatened.

Profiles of Classic Roles Played by Children

The Hero

My function in the family: I am the rescuer and surrogate parent. I am responsible, serious, controlling, ambitious, and industrious; I cover for the alcohol problems and entangled relationships by taking over the parental role when others are unable to do what is needed. I sacrifice time and compassion for myself in favor of meeting everyone else's needs—I always come last. I am perfectionistic and elevate my family's level of functioning.

What I long for deep inside: I want others to take responsibility and relieve me of it. I also want to be seen for who I am and not what I do.

My greatest fears: When I let go, chaos will ensue. Others won't be able to get along without my help.

How the role carries over into my adulthood: Poorly policed boundaries, poor self-care. Overworked. Inclined to give unsolicited advice or help. Bad at listening. At risk for stress and burnout. At the risk of marrying someone with an addiction problem. Feelings of guilt.

Unique, positive potential: Good leadership, independent, able to take responsibility, industrious, capable, engaged.

The Scapegoat

My function: I direct negative attention away from the drinking and the person with the addiction by being a problem child and providing a target for the family's pent-up frustrations.

What I long for deep inside: To be seen for who I am, to receive justice and recognition for everything I do that is good.

My biggest fears: That I am cursed somehow and that I attract misfortune and problems. That whatever I do is doomed to fail.

How the role carries over into my adulthood: Difficulty relaxing, late to engage and develop potential, difficulty finishing projects, at risk for creating drama and insecurity in close relationships.

Unique, positive potential: Honesty, bravery, ability to understand people who are different, the nerve to take risks, accommodating, humble, independent.

The Forgotten Child

My function in the family: I provide some relief to my parents by not demanding time and attention, not getting in the way, taking care of myself, and being an "easy" child.

What I long for deep inside: That people will take an interest in me, that my opinion will be valued as much as everyone else's, to know and feel that I am worthy.

My biggest fears: That no one will miss me if I'm not around, that I am not worthwhile company, that if I attract your attention, I won't be able to retain it, that I will create problems.

How the role carries over into my adulthood: Indecisive and phlegmatic, anxious, immersed in a specific area of interest—very often to the point of being an expert—or all-consuming hobby. I am often physically sick. Disempowered and without stamina. I disappear in large groups and bond with only a few people or a pet.

Unique, positive potential: Imaginative and creative, original, interesting, independent, artistically gifted.

The Clown

My function in the family: I alleviate ill-humor and negative moods to bring my parents back together when they clash and break the ice when there's a tense silence. I generally try to smooth over the rough spots.

What I long for deep inside: To understand exactly what is going on, that others will take responsibility for their own feelings and moods, to have permission to cry and get angry.

My biggest fears: If I don't get others to laugh, the family will break up. I fear that problems will arise that can't be solved. It is hard to be present for a difficult conversation because I am afraid of others being in a bad mood and becoming angry or sad.

How the role carries over into my adulthood: Nervous, attention-seeking, inclined to avoid conflict, manic. I've always got one foot out the door.

Unique, positive potential: Entertaining and fun, extroverted, upbeat company, responsive, charming, buoyant.

Identifying Your Own Role(s)

Becoming an expert at knowing and being yourself requires attention, courage, curiosity, and patience. As you begin to identify the role that predominantly determines your behavior, the descriptions below of typical situations may help you recognize or clarify the responsibilities you bore in your family, and that may have burdened you ever since. These roles represent functions that your parents should have borne, and it may be difficult to convince yourself that the roles are not who you are but rather an identity you took on to survive for reasons over which you had no control.

Scenario 1: Your mother is calling, and as soon as you hear her voice on the phone, you know she has been drinking.

Ways of responding:

1. *The Hero:* You get upset and start asking her how much she has drunk and why. You then arrange to go to her, to try and manage the chaos you think she is in. On the way to her house, you stop at the supermarket and buy some food and other items that you recently noticed she was short on.

2. *The Scapegoat:* You get angry and terminate the conversation, saying you do not want to talk to her because she is drunk.

3. *The Forgotten Child:* You pretend nothing's wrong and talk with her a little while. You let her determine when the conversation will end.

4. *The Clown:* Pitying your mother as you chat with her, you try to cheer her up with some jokes. You feel some satisfaction when you make her forget about herself and get her to laugh with you.

5. *THE HEALTHY ALTERNATIVE:* You say immediately: "Mom, I can hear that you've been drinking, so I'm hanging up now. We can talk again one day when you're sober." You hang up.

Scenario 2: Your parents are unhappy that you have not visited for a long time.

1. *The Hero:* You feel guilty and quickly check your calendar to find a date when you can visit. You feel a duty and a great responsibility for their well-being; they are your parents. You may also suggest that they call your siblings since you resent having done so much to fulfill your parents' needs.

2. *The Scapegoat:* You take the blame personally and are irritated by the implied guilt on your part. You don't see why you should feel guilty, given how unpleasant and difficult being around them can be. You do not follow up on their "invitation" to visit.

3. *The Forgotten Child:* Their sadness makes you uncomfortable, so instead of reacting honestly, you try to make nice. They suggest a date for you to come, and you answer that that might work out, but you say it primarily to avoid conflict.

4. *The Clown:* Sensitive to their feelings of sadness and disappointment, you hurry to say nice, funny things. You promise to come soon.

5. *THE HEALTHY ALTERNATIVE:* You listen to them and acknowledge that you understand their frustration at not having seen much of you. You also regret that they put the blame on you. You explain that you would like to see them and that you miss being able to be together, but it won't be possible for you as long as their lives are guided by their alcohol problems. The drinking makes visiting them unpredictable and unsafe for you—you never know what to expect when you arrive, and you do not want to expose yourself to that. The day you all can talk about that problem, it may be different.

Scenario 3: Your parents criticize one of your siblings for never coming to visit.

1. *The Hero:* You feel tremendous discomfort over your parents' pain. You comfort them and promise that you will try to get in touch with the sibling. You call him immediately, explaining that your parents are pained by the fact that he never visits and that maybe he ought to think more about others and less about himself.

2. *The Scapegoat:* You think—and perhaps say—that this is their situation to remedy, and you do not want to be caught up in their conflicts.

3. *The Forgotten Child:* You feel horrible and want to get away. You chat with your parents in a way that does not stir up tension and unpleasant emotions, and you end the conversation as soon as possible. As soon as you hang up, you turn on the TV, start playing a game, etc.

4. *The Clown:* You feel discomfort and tension over the negative feelings, and you immediately try to lighten up the conversation with a funny story about something you just experienced. You want more than anything in the world to put them in a better mood, and you feel pride and joy when they start laughing at your story and the mood changes.

5. *THE HEALTHY ALTERNATIVE:* You say, in acknowledgment of the situation, that it must be uncomfortable to feel that your child is pulling away from you, and you can understand their pain, but you will not talk about your siblings behind their backs. You repeat the message if necessary.

Scenario 4: You visit your parents, only to find your father drunk on the couch and your mother sitting in the kitchen, crying.

1. *The Hero:* First, despite your anger, you go into the living room and help your father to bed. You then sit down and try to comfort your mother. The two of you talk for a long time about what your father has done and said, and you see how unhappy she is. You promise her that you will speak to your father when he wakes up. Afterward, you search the house for bottles and pour out all the alcohol you find.

2. *The Scapegoat:* You turn around and leave the house, slamming the door behind you, enraged at another failed attempt to do the right thing. You seethe with anger at not being able to count on them, and you hate them for it. Once again, they have wasted your time, and you feel they do not care about you.

3. *The Forgotten Child:* You slide past your father as if he weren't there, and then your mother, and you sit down and turn on the TV or check your phone. You feel uneasy, but you're used to it; all you can do is try to think of something else.

4. *The Clown:* You sit down with your mother and try everything you can to cheer her up and distract her. You assure her that everything will get better, and your father will soon straighten himself out.

5. *THE HEALTHY ALTERNATIVE:* You put a blanket over your father and hug your mother and tell her you're leaving. If she starts to apply emotional pressure, you remind her that as an adult, she is responsible for her life. Say that, as her child, you cannot talk to her about your father or her marital problems, but you know a place where she can get help, and you would love to give her information about it. You leave.

Scenario 5: You do not hear from the parent who has an addiction for an unusually long time.

1. *The Hero:* You try, unsuccessfully, to reach them numerous times, and it worries you so much that you cannot sleep at night. You envision various disasters that may have befallen them, and you wonder what you should do. Soon your inner turmoil and guilt get so severe that you set your work and your own family aside to get your parents' situation under control.

2. *The Scapegoat:* You try to care, but the fact is, the trust between you and your parents is broken no matter what. You don't feel obligated to do anything, but you are angry at them nevertheless for once again stirring up trouble in your life.

3. *The Forgotten Child:* You feel uneasy, but you don't take any initiative in the situation. As you wait for your parents to reestablish contact, you try to mask your discomfort by forcing yourself to think cheerful thoughts.

4. *The Clown:* You send some funny messages and cute pictures to your parents, and hope the situation clears up soon.

5. THE HEALTHY ALTERNATIVE: You know that alcohol abuse destroys relationships, and you remind yourself that what is going on is not your fault in any way. You also know how stubbornly reluctant people with addictions can be in seeking help. If you tried to confront the drinking problem head-on, your parents would surely try to deny and normalize it. Instead of focusing exclusively on them, you seek out someone you can talk to and try to deal with your own feelings. Perhaps you join a group for other adult children of alcoholics, where you will find proof that you are not the only person in this situation. You have taken the responsibility to learn how alcoholism works, and you take comfort in understanding that you are not to blame.

Scenario 6: You, your partner, and your children go to visit your father. When you arrive, you realize that he is drunk, even though he has agreed not to drink in front of your children.

1. *The Hero:* You feel great disappointment and frustration but cannot express it because it's too hard on your father. You try as hard as possible to smooth things over so everything will look like a normal family visit. Your compassion takes over, and you start doing things that need doing around the house—cooking, for example. When your partner says it's time to go home, you get angry with her because, you say, your children need to know their grandfather.

2. *The Scapegoat:* You immediately leave, telling your father that you are angry and disappointed that he has not adhered to such a simple agreement. You do not initiate contact with him again.

3. *The Forgotten Child:* You pretend nothing's wrong and stay all day, all the while trying to minimize conflict. You downplay the whole situation, so there is no conflict between you and your partner.

4. *The Clown:* You stick around and try to fill the room with good cheer and laughter as if you could prevent everyone from noticing the tension and embarrassment.

5. *THE HEALTHY ALTERNATIVE:* You assess your father's condition in terms of whether you can talk to him or not. If he's too drunk, you simply say you're going home, and you leave. If he is still coherent, you tell him you can see that he has been drinking and that, in line with your agreement, you will not be around him in that situation. You know there is no sense in discussing important matters with someone under the influence, and you tell him you will contact him one day when he is sober. After leaving with your family, you talk to your partner and your

children about what was wrong and acknowledge everyone's experience and their feelings about the situation, and come up with an alternative family activity. If you are very sad or disappointed yourself, you resolve to find someone understanding to talk to about the problem.

Scenario 7: *Your mother is abusing alcohol. Everyone is now aware of this, and she knows it herself.*

1. *The Hero:* You feel terribly sorry for her, and you want to do everything you can to improve her life, so she stops drinking. You believe that you are partially at fault, that if you had only done more for her, this wouldn't have happened. The situation leaves you feeling stressed and with a bad conscience. You think a lot about her during the day at work, and when you get home, you can be irritable with or absent from your own family because you feel so wrung-out and tired. Deep inside, you're unsure whether she's actually addicted to alcohol or instead simply has a hard time managing her life, and you think maybe you can help her with that.

2. *The Scapegoat:* You often feel anger and disappointment when you think of your mother, but you've begun living your own life, and the two of you no longer have anything in common. You don't intend to have much to do with her anymore, and since you want to protect your children from getting disappointed by her, you don't intend to let them see her much either.

3. *The Forgotten Child:* You do not quite know what is at the root of your mother's problems. You come to visit when she asks, but it can be uncomfortable once in a while because she just sits and cries or seems distant. Even when you want to get far away from her, you do not say anything because you don't want to add to her troubles.

4. *The Clown:* You know that you and your mother have a special connection—she often lights up when you enter the room—and you feel as if you can make her happy. You think she drinks because she has had a hard life or suffers from depression. You are often able to cheer her up, and you think that, given a chance, you might be able to make her happy enough to stop drinking and begin to take care of herself.

5. *THE HEALTHY ALTERNATIVE:* You seek help in addressing the wounds and scars that your own upbringing left you with, and you don't shy away from discussing your mother's alcohol abuse with your siblings. But you also make sure that she is not the only conversation topic when you meet. You and your siblings investigate the possibility of your mother getting into treatment.

Two Questions About Your Roles

Which statement best reflects your role regarding your family's alcohol problems?

1. *The Hero:* If I do not do anything, everything will go off the rails. It is my duty to help my family when there are problems. I feel sorry for Mom and Dad. They are my parents, and they count on me, but I am strong.

2. *The Scapegoat:* I do not want anything to do with them. They do not care about anyone, and they betray everyone. That's what they've always done, and they will continue to do it. I don't mean anything to them anyway—they have always cared more about my siblings than me. I may have been a fairly difficult child, which did not make it easier for my parents, so maybe I'm also partly to blame. (That's what I have been told, anyway.) Maybe I'm just too big a handful for some people. In any case, things typically go wrong if I am involved.

3. *The Forgotten Child:* There's nothing I can say or do that will help, so it doesn't matter that much whether I'm here or not. If I just stay calm, it will pass.

4. *The Clown:* Who wouldn't want to drink if they were so sad all the time? I feel a great responsibility for others' happiness and well-being, and I feel that I have an especially deep connection with my parents. They are happier when I'm with them—my dose of cheer makes a difference.

5. *THE HEALTHY OUTLOOK:* My family's alcohol problem is not my fault, and it can be very difficult to remedy. Thanks to my knowledge about addiction, I am able to take care of myself so I do not become entangled or enmeshed. Cultivating strong and healthy relationships elsewhere will help make up for what my parents failed to provide and generally help me look out for myself. Perhaps my parents' problem will never be solved, but I will take care of myself and live a good life. I'm worth it, and that's what I deserve.

EXERCISES: BREAK OUT OF YOUR ROLES

1. Have You Played Along?

Describe some specific situations in which you have felt, thought, or reacted in a way that obviously matched one of the four roles. Be conscious of the feelings that arise as you work with each question.

What are the feelings associated with your role?

What response do you get from your family when you are in your role?

As an adult, how do you see yourself and the role you have had to play?

Breaking loose from the role you assumed and its perceived responsibilities starts with fully realizing that it's a wild goose chase and that, no matter how hard you try, your contribution/actions in that role will never solve the problem. Answer the following questions honestly.

How many attempts, over how many years, have you made in that role to help improve your family's situation?

What do you think it would take for you to shed that role?

How would it feel to no longer take the same amount and kind of responsibility?

What would you like for yourself when you no longer have to fulfill that role?

2. Finding Your Way Out

Create a plan you will follow to ease yourself out of your recognized role in the family. Resolve to strengthen yourself, be extra-aware of your own genuine thoughts and feelings—not the ones you would automatically expect of the role—and be at the forefront of taking care of and being responsible for yourself. Draw up some guidelines for how you will operate independently of the role when you are required to be with your parents and siblings. Remind yourself that even if you are pressured to step back into your role, it can only occur if you let it happen. You have the power to change yourself into the person you want to be.

Recognize the pain that alcohol abuse has put you through, but also your fear of what will happen if you stop taking responsibility for your parents. Say to yourself, "Alcohol abuse is a disease that afflicts my mother/father, and they are not themselves. It's not my fault, and it's not in my power to prevent it. Since they could not and cannot take care of me, I have to take care of myself, and I will. I deserve the best."

EXERCISE: WRITE YOUR LIFE STORY

Adulthood, Part 1

Let the questions below guide you as you write the next part of your life story.

At what age did you begin taking responsibility for things that your parents still ought to have been managing for you?

How old were you when you left your childhood home and became independent from your parents?

What were the circumstances in which you left your childhood home?

What would you call the milestones—positive and negative—of your adult life? Have you experienced significant losses as an adult?

11

PUTTING THE BRAKES ON UNHEALTHY INVOLVEMENT

Being over-involved with other people and not having confidence that they can manage for themselves is called *codependency*. It varies by degree and can range from a slight tendency to a need so extreme that a person finds it difficult or impossible to function without having a person with a problem or an addiction to take care of.

People who develop intensely enmeshed and codependent relationships cannot take full responsibility for themselves or stay focused on themselves. Instead, their responsibility is channeled into someone *else's* finances, health, employment, perhaps even how much they drink. It may also manifest itself in a compulsive need for a perfectly trimmed hedge, an always shiny and clean car, and everything perfectly maintained. Either way, at the heart of it is a craving for control, to keep things running in the face of instability deep below the surface, and a need to fend off fear.

In relationships that are based on codependency, even the other person's *feelings* are considered fair game for control. You may try to protect them in every possible way, even being unable to say no to them for fear that you will upset them. Or maybe you'll choose to avoid discussing a problem because you do not trust them to be able to handle it—another form of control.

For someone raised in a home shaped by alcohol addiction, codependency can be rooted in traumatic experiences from childhood, from harsh scoldings to liquor-fueled accidents to threats of suicide or finding a parent unconscious. Codependency can run in families and be passed on from generation to generation.

Actions driven by codependency can be based on expectations about how the person with an addiction—or the world at large—operates that aren't actually borne out by facts. Such misconceptions can take on lives of their own, running around and around in your head, serving all the while as distractions from and veils over the real, underlying problems.

If on the surface, everything appears to be meticulously maintained and thoroughly attended to, you can tell yourself that everything is under effective control. At their essence, interactions based on codependency maintain a facade that allows problems and unhealthy situations to continue unabated. On the other side of the same coin, being overly engaged in the pain, sadness, and troubles of others can also deflect the focus from the core problem.

"I am 41 years old and still, in my adult life, constantly on guard. I find it hard to trust the people around me. I am unsure of myself and others—what are they thinking? I run from conflict. I say yes to too much, even to things I do not want to do. I am a people-pleaser and a yes-man. My self-respect is very low."—Mona

Codependent involvement is a misconceived expansion of a parental role, and it is a common impulse behind the behavior of both the Hero and Clown roles. Both attempt to remedy a situation in their own way. The Scapegoat does this too, but on an emotional level, by absorbing the pain and sorrow in the air until the day they reach their limit. The emotions that someone co-dependently enmeshed feels are intense: bad conscience, fear of something going wrong, strong feelings of compassion, and a desire to help and protect.

What Over-involvement Does to Your Life and the Lives of Others

Becoming overly involved in your parents' lives is like having an extra child. Driving them to appointments, rushing to rescue them from every crisis—all this can be disruptive to your own family, and the seeming monopoly that your parents have on your attention can leave your partner feeling frustrated and let down. His or her efforts to defend and support you may lead to direct conflict with your parents, which can have serious consequences for your own household.

Going all-out for a parent, a child, or a partner, even when they do not need it and haven't asked for it, may indicate good intentions but actually be a very destructive form of help. Tying a child's shoelaces even though he is perfectly capable of doing it himself, or cleaning up his room instead of teaching him to do it, gets in the way of healthy growth and life experiences that lead to autonomy and independence. You may be inadvertently teaching a kind of helplessness that will interfere with him achieving his highest potential.

Codependent interactions also come at the expense of your self-care, and they help keep you always at the very bottom of your own list of priorities. Trapped in a savior mindset, you miss out on your own life and face unending demands. For all your composed, capable, and hardworking qualities, you can find it difficult to ask for something for yourself and accept care and recognition from others.

You may begin to tolerate things you would not have tolerated before: your father driving drunk, maybe even with your kids in the car, your mother lying, etc. You stretch yourself too far, to the point where you barely recognize yourself. That can open the door to rage and fear or leave you utterly tapped out and burned out. Your own children may end up at the losing end of such misplaced priorities.

Am I Not Allowed to Help?

Because it is human nature to be compassionate and important to take care of and support others, it can be confusing to sort out which kind of help is healthy and which is overly involved in an unhealthy way. But once you can start distinguishing between the two and can consciously choose the healthy kind, you will reduce the worries and anxiety that have been behind your need to help. Your nerves can begin to settle, enabling you to get in better touch with yourself, giving you a chance to be more present in your own life.

In the long run, this will provide you with clarity that makes it easier to determine exactly what you have the power to change and what you don't. You will find that channeling energy into things you actually can change means basing your actions on groundedness and awareness rather than impulsivity. The result will be that the support you offer can be deeply nurturing and transformative for yourself and others. And your actions will neither interfere with the efforts of others nor prevent them from reaching the goals they may have set for themselves.

Your Own Lane

"Staying in your own lane" will bring results from the moment you begin investing in yourself. Your life will begin to shape itself more in accordance with your own needs and who you authentically are. This healing process is activated when you stop investing all your resources in something that will not change. Once you give up your habit of being on call at all times, your possibilities will expand; the people around you will see a happy person who is thriving and taking care of herself.

Obviously, you must expect a change as momentous as giving up a codependent behavior to be more complex than simply turning off your phone. Yes, you will begin to flourish when you choose to stop being involved with others in unhealthy ways, but you may also feel grief or pain of some sort. The prospect of losing your longtime identity as the good, helpful person who sacrificed everything may bring fear and guilt along with it. You may initially feel an emptiness in the inner space that was once taken up by your laser focus on the person with the problems.

Dare to give those feelings an airing—bring them out where you can see them clearly. For one thing, this investment you make in yourself will help guarantee that you no longer experience emptiness, sadness, or disappointment over the dependent person's failure to reciprocate your care. Consider this honesty a tool for finding your authentic self.

Keep in mind that your whole family situation won't suddenly change around you just because of your changed outlook. Lots of familiar things, both comfortable and uncomfortable, will continue to play out. You might find that your father, for example, doesn't react in any way: Maybe he thinks he is managing just fine without you, and in any case, he never really acknowledged all your sacrifices for his sake anyway. He may even think it's high time you focused more on your own family than on him.

Alternatively, he may assume the stance of a victim. Or perhaps, once things have changed, your mother will try to blame you for her loneliness, complaining that you and your family never come to see her anymore. She may decide she has no reason to pull herself together because you're going to ignore her anyway. On the other hand, she may be relieved that you aren't keeping watch anymore because that will provide her with more opportunities to drink.

As you hear all this and feel that powerful old urge to intervene, try something new: Be thoughtful about it but sit on your hands. Prepare to respond with answers that are something other than an automatic yes. How about "I need to think it over—I'll get back to you," for instance?

Through it all, allow yourself to find out how you feel. What feels good, and what feels bad? Engage in an inner dialogue. Ask yourself, "What is this all about? Can I do something else? Should I help in this case or not?" Confer with your partner about what would work best for the two of you. The key is not to jump right in but rather to give yourself permission to take time to consider. Instead of acting reflexively, tune in to your inner signals about whether something makes sense or not.

And begin, in daily life, practicing the firm and balanced delivery of **no**.

EXERCISES: ADDRESSING YOUR UNHEALTHY INVOLVEMENT

1. How Overly Involved Are You?

Check each statement that applies to you.

___I sometimes deny how bad things are with my mother/father/partner's drinking.

___In general, I find it difficult to say no.

___I periodically worry a great deal about my mother's/father's/partner's problems.

___I often do everything possible to help others at the expense of meeting my own needs.

___I am often in emotional turmoil because of my parent's/partner's alcohol problems.

___My mood is easily affected by how others feel.

___I find it difficult to enjoy most situations because I am always expecting something to go wrong.

___I feel guilty and responsible when things don't go well for others.

___I give a lot of advice because I think I am capable of solving other people's problems.

___I generally put a lot of demands on myself.

___I think I can make a difference concerning my mother's/father's/partner's abuse.

___I can be very critical and judgmental of myself.

___Deep down inside, I feel weak and inadequate.

___I find it hard to ask for help and support from others.

___I lie to others about how things are going.

___I think I have to be strong and manage everything myself.

___I find it difficult to know what I am feeling.

___*I feel guilty when I do something good for myself.*

___*I have difficulty setting boundaries because I am unsure of what is normal.*

___*I often help and talk to others about their problems but keep my own problems to myself.*

If you recognize more than five of these statements as accurate descriptions of yourself, then you most likely have developed codependent patterns and have assumed a rescuing role.

2. Letting Go of Over-involvement

A. Sit on Your Hands

Take the title of this exercise seriously—it also constitutes the complete set of instructions. It is about not *rushing around and doing everything in the kitchen, picking up the laundry, balancing others' accounts. When you're with people you love, you must learn to be idle, to be present but let others do some of what needs to be done. In a compulsive caring role, you act without assessing whether it is necessary or your rightful place. Your goal in this next learning period is not to jump in to do or arrange things for others. You must let your family come and share in practical household tasks, so you also have free time and can take breaks. You must train yourself to be with others without doing anything. Shifting from unhealthy behaviors and thinking is not done with a single snap of the fingers. It will take time to change, but it is possible and necessary if you want to break out of abusive patterns in your childhood family.*

B. Become Aware of Your Codependent Patterns

Perhaps you've always felt it was your responsibility to help everyone else, and you struggle to take care of yourself and set healthy limits. This pattern is deeply ingrained in you, and it seems like a part of you; anything different feels unimaginable. But it is time now for you to break out of these automatic patterns of feeling and acting.

Try to recall the last several times you took too much responsibility for someone else. Briefly describe those occasions. How does that behavior look to you from here and now? What kind of feelings arise in you when you think about those situations?

Feeling anger, grief, and powerlessness here may indicate that your care, actions, and love have not had the result you intended. Anger and powerlessness are natural feelings that a person who is overly involved often suppresses. Those feelings are important to take note of. They are an understandable and genuine response to having wasted so much energy helping someone who did not take responsibility for themselves and who did not get better.

(If you don't sense any emotions emerging, it may be because you have shut down your feelings and rendered them inaccessible. That is a situation that responds best to working with other people: It would be very helpful to you to seek either an adult child of alcoholics support group or a therapist, to help you get in touch with your feelings.)

Reflecting on these most recent instances mentioned above, try to imagine how they would have unfolded if you had taken 100% responsibility for yourself and acknowledged that you did not have the time or resources to help out. Imagine how that might have affected both you and the other person(s) involved.

If you have been reluctant to let go for a long time, notice whether you feel any guilt and whether you have trouble accepting the idea that it is okay to let go. Being able to let go is your goal, even at the cost of a bad conscience. That bad conscience is not permanent; you will notice that saying no gradually gets easier and easier. Once you truly feel that no *inside, you will no longer be in any doubt that you are on the right track. Take this as your signal that, even though others in your environment may face major challenges in matters of responsibility and self-care, you now can and should take care of yourself.*

C. The Staircase to Freedom

Draw a stairway with four or five steps. Beginning at the bottom, from the smallest, least scary challenge up to the largest, scariest one, assign each step some kind of overly involved behavior or a situation in which the people are enmeshed that you feel you could change if you put your mind to it. Make the first one something you could accomplish fairly easily, then challenge your comfort zone a little more with each ascending step. The top step should signify taking loving care of yourself and breaking away from all kinds of unhealthy involvement or entanglement.

As you fill in each of the steps, think about how you might encourage and support yourself along the way. Formulate a plan: Set a target date or timeline for each step, and think of how to reward yourself at every new step (e.g., getting a massage, seeing a movie with a friend, making your favorite dish, taking a trip you've dreamt of for a long time).

EXERCISE: WRITE YOUR LIFE STORY

Adulthood, Part 2

Let the questions below guide you as you write the next part of your life story.

If you have children, how has becoming a parent been for you?

How have your intimate relationships been?

How has your professional life been?

What do your finances look like?

How is your relationship with your parents today? Do they still drink?

What kind of relationships do you have with your siblings now?

12

SAY GOODBYE TO DRAMA IN RELATIONSHIPS

THE DRAMA TRIANGLE

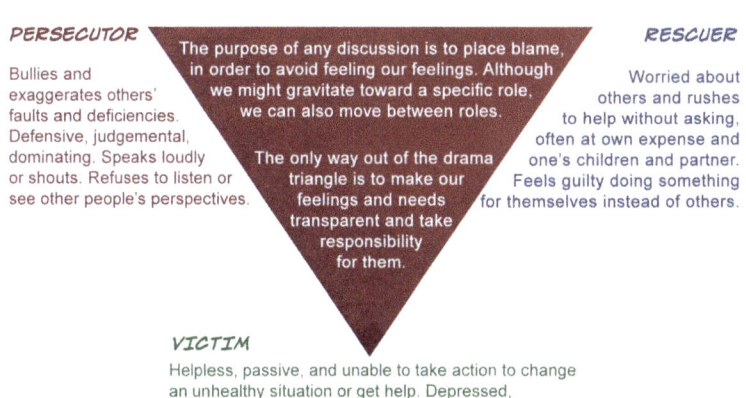

PERSECUTOR
Bullies and exaggerates others' faults and deficiencies. Defensive, judgemental, dominating. Speaks loudly or shouts. Refuses to listen or see other people's perspectives.

The purpose of any discussion is to place blame, in order to avoid feeling our feelings. Although we might gravitate toward a specific role, we can also move between roles.

The only way out of the drama triangle is to make our feelings and needs transparent and take responsibility for them.

RESCUER
Worried about others and rushes to help without asking, often at own expense and one's children and partner. Feels guilty doing something for themselves instead of others.

VICTIM
Helpless, passive, and unable to take action to change an unhealthy situation or get help. Depressed, self-critical, with feelings of guilt and shame and doubt. Unable to set clear boundaries. Indecisive.

The triangle shown here illustrates a dysfunctional way of communicating. *Dysfunctional* means *malfunctioning*, which applies to the kind of communication depicted here because it never gets to the heart of the matter and therefore never accomplishes anything.

PERSECUTOR	VICTIM	RESCUER
"I'm OK, but you're not. It is always your fault. I am the one who knows what's really going on, so you'd better do what I say." "You'd drive anybody to drink." "You think you're perfect, don't you?" "Get out of my way, I am sick and tired of listening to you." or "(A relative of someone with an addiction) "You've been drinking again!" "You're the biggest loser I know." "Pull yourself together. You're an ugly mess."	Everyone is OK, except for me. No matter how hard I try, I can never get things right. I need someone to do it for me. When people find out who I really am, they abandon me. Bad things always happen to me. "How could you take away my stash when you know what I am going through?" "I hate myself. I always screw things up." "You're wasting your time with me. I'll never be able to pull out of this." "No one really gets it, I can't take it anymore. I'm going to end it all." "I don't know who I am anymore." or "How could you do this to me when you know what I am going through?" "My life has been ruined, and things are never going to get any better." "Why me? Why do I always end up with someone who treats me like this?" "I can't do it on my own. I am such an idiot." "I just can't decide -- it's always so hard to make a decision."	I'm OK. You're not. People need me. I'm nice and I can fix you. Without me, everything would go off the rails. Dependent's statements "I'm never going to drink again." "From now on, everything is going to be perfect." "We'll do something wonderful to celebrate your birthday, I promise." "You'll never see me get in a fight again. I've learned my lesson." or Family member "Don't you worry, I've got this covered." "I'm always here for you." "I'll bail you out -- it can come out of my pocket." "I've called your boss and got the rest of the week off for you. I know what you're going through."

This communication and behavioral dynamic is called the *drama triangle*. The *drama* has to do with avoiding unbearable emotions and not being left with the blame and responsibility for whatever bad situation you are talking about.

The dynamics of the triangle can be very fluid. You may start as the Rescuer and then suddenly be shuffled by a burst of anger or badly handled pressure to the position of Persecutor. Or a Victim who doesn't get the help and recognition she longs for might suddenly shift into the Persecutor's role. Participants may cycle through the roles of victim, offender, and savior, sometimes very rapidly (though they often have a preferred role).

These three roles get acted out as the participants all seek to get out from under any potential responsibility for their own needs. In relationships where asking for care or attention is unsafe, a kind of game develops that guarantees no needs will be met, apart from indirectly.

The Rescuer helps and gives good advice (even when it hasn't been requested), sacrifices, takes responsibility, and takes care of other people's duties.

The Persecutor criticizes and makes others feel uncomfortable. He is aggressive and judicial. The Persecutor blames others and perceives himself as real but without responsibility for the drama and the problems.

The Victim blames herself and is unhappy, convinced she doesn't have the same resources, opportunities, money, time, effort, health, etc., as everyone else and therefore can't do anything about her terrible situation, no matter how hard she tries.

So, how, exactly, does the drama triangle work? Here's a sample scenario:

Mom is tipsy when the rest of the family arrives home. They're expecting dinner, but there is no dinner. She had promised to cook so the oldest daughter could go to an evening class, and now her failure makes her feel ashamed and angry and inadequate. Suddenly, she spills over with rage. "I never have any time to myself," she thinks. "They're a bunch of vampires who suck the life out of me, leaving me drained and with no energy left to do anything for myself. I never have time to catch up." (Persecutor)

Now her daughter will miss her class, and Mom feels overwhelmed by regret at not keeping her commitment and doing what she said she'd do. She blames herself. "I'm a bad mother. I'm such a loser—a miserable excuse for a human being." (Victim)

She goes out to the kitchen, but rather than starting to cook, she collapses in self-pity. Seeing her daughter enter the kitchen, she sits down and starts crying. (Victim)

"What is wrong, Mom?" the daughter asks, trying to alleviate her mother's discomfort. (Rescuer)

"Everything has gone to hell," Mom says, "and I can't take it anymore. I'm just not up to it, and you are all better off without me." (Victim)

These words leave the daughter scared and upset, and she begins to worry that her mother might try to hurt herself. Instead of making it clear to Mom that she is angry about not making it to class, she displaces that anger with expressions of concern and love. "You shouldn't feel that way, Mom," she says, driven now to do everything she can to make her mother feel good again. "I love you, and you are the best mom in the world. Here, let me help you make dinner." (Rescuer)

Dad comes into the kitchen. It's immediately clear to him that Mom has been drinking, and he feels cheated, let down. "Have you been drinking again?" he asks. "We had a deal! Why can't you keep a simple goddamn agreement? You can't even follow through on something as simple as cooking dinner!" (Persecutor)

She replies, "You have no right to talk. You're never home anyway. You don't care about us—we mean nothing to you." (Persecutor)

The tension continues. At the end of the evening, the daughter goes to bed very sad. She can see that the adults don't treat each other very well, and she feels alone in having to cope with everything. She never has any time for her own things. (Victim) But if she didn't keep up, she believes everything would fall apart. (Rescuer)

...and so, the drama triangle continues endlessly. No problems are ever solved, no growth ever happens.

A drama triangle has no place in a healthy family setting. First and foremost, it is a negative way of relating to the world, but it's also a destructive way of seeing oneself. There is an exaggerated focus on the wrongdoing and who is to blame. There are never any winners here; it's a race to the bottom in which all the players end up feeling bad. No matter where you sit in the triangle, the interactions will never be equal or healthy. Depending on which of the roles you play, there will always be either too much responsibility or no responsibility at all.

As long as you find yourself caught up in the drama triangle, nothing will be solved—the only possible outcome is a standoff, or worse. Making yourself aware that there is such a structure, however, will reduce your risk of getting trapped in it. It may take some time to wrest yourself from its grip but acknowledging its existence must come first.

"The worst thing wasn't the shame, but the guilt that I often felt. From the time I was very young, my father was always initiating some kind of competition with me. He took advantage of my being very shy and made me feel guilty about myself. When I was nine, he told me it was my own fault I had no friends—what a nice thing to say to a child who is being relentlessly bullied in school! I felt another layer of guilt for not being able to protect my mother."—Lina

· · ·

How Do You Know You're in the Drama Triangle?

One indication that you may be caught up in the drama triangle is that everything relating to emotions is jumbled up. There is no sign of clear, authentic feelings, but rather the overall effect is exhausting, provoking, hurtful, inflexible, and scary. Even feelings of care, love, and helpfulness are mixed up and confused. There is discomfort because the triangle infringes on individual boundaries; there's hopelessness. Old patterns seem to repeat and repeat, but nothing goes anywhere; there's anger and anxiety because you feel that everything will fall apart if you withdraw from the triangle.

Another hallmark of the drama triangle is the refusal of one party to recognize and take responsibility for her own behavior while blaming someone else. Phrases like, *You said,* and *You did* crop up frequently, and generalizations like *always*, *never*, *all the time*, and *nobody* are common.

The pull of the drama triangle is powerful and very hard to resist, drawing people into conflicts that nobody can win.

EXERCISE: YOUR PART IN THE DRAMA TRIANGLE

Close your eyes and recall some of the drama triangles you have been caught in. Describe some of these experiences. What was the mood or tone of these situations? What kind of feelings do you associate with them?

Continue with the following questions:

In which situations do you typically enter into the drama triangle? And with whom?

What is the primary role you tend to assume in the drama triangle—do you typically end up as Persecutor, Rescuer, or Victim? What purpose do you think that role serves for you? Is there something you are trying to avoid taking responsibility for by assuming this particular role again and again?

Why would you like to get out of the drama triangle?

What do you think will happen if you don't play the part?

Is there something more responsible and appropriate that you could do for yourself than participating in the drama triangle (e.g., being honest about your needs, thoughts, and feelings; avoiding taking responsibility for the feelings and situations of others; observing people who seem to be good at taking responsibility for themselves)?

What do you anticipate to be your most significant challenges in breaking out of someone else's drama triangle?

EXERCISE: WRITE YOUR LIFE STORY

Follow-Up

Once you have completed your life story, ask yourself the following questions:

Are there problematic issues in your life that continue to repeat themselves?

Is there a disadvantageous pattern in your way of being or relating to other people, especially people you have known throughout your life?

Perhaps you recognize some of your current problems as being the same ones you had as a child. For example, are you so unsure about other people that you often feel different from them, or maybe you find yourself giving a lot but getting nothing in return?

Once you have written your life story, you will have the opportunity to get in closer touch with how things really were during periods you might have forgotten about. Through your work with your story, the details can begin to emerge. Read it through, noting how it affects you emotionally. Try to see yourself from an objective point of view. Sometimes looking at photos of yourself from the specific periods you are reading about can make it easier to see yourself from the outside.

Now that you've written your entire story, do you see your history any differently? Has your overall sense of your story changed in the process of writing it down? Are there any particular passages you reacted strongly to?

Once your story is completed, don't abandon it. Continue to revisit and add to it, staying curious about recollecting even more of your earlier life. Be aware that you'll continue to encounter many old moods and emotions along the way. If you work especially intensely on it, you may experience some emotional swings and sometimes feel deeply affected and vulnerable. That is quite understandable and as it should be. Be compassionate and understanding with yourself as you do the work. In the long run, it will help make you more aware of your essence—you will begin to feel yourself more clearly—and that is precisely the goal.

13

YOU HAVE THE RIGHT...

You have the right to say what you think, the right to make mistakes, the right to be who you are. Your rights are what you think you deserve, which will determine not only how you interact with other people but also how you see your own value in relation to them.

Your rights are also linked to your self-esteem. When you have a strong sense of self-worth, you find it easier to assert the rights you deserve. And when it comes to both self-worth and rights, it is important to set the bar high.

Growing up in a household where boundaries are indistinct, and uncertainty is common can make it harder as an adult to realize that you even *have* fundamental rights. But you do, and you must be perfectly clear about them in your mind.

You have the right...

...to have experiences and invest them with meaning.

All people experience the world from their own perspective; there is no single objective truth. The fact that your experiences, feelings, and thoughts are yours alone makes them no less worthy or less valid.

...to feel what you feel.

Feelings are feelings. They aren't there to be debated but to be respected. (However, this does not mean that your feelings may dominate others.)

...to be yourself, to be who you are.

When it comes to articulating your thoughts, feelings, and needs, you are on an equal footing with everyone else. You are just as interesting and important and valuable as any other human being. It is your right to express your own opinion, even if others do not agree with it or understand it.

...to say no.

You have the right *not* to live up to other people's expectations or needs and to ask others to stop abusive behavior. You have the right to be caring toward and responsible for yourself. You are not responsible for other people's feelings unless, of course, you violate them or disrespect them. You also have the right to change your mind and make mistakes without feeling shame or guilt.

...to take care of your body as you see fit, and ask for help, advice, care, and understanding.

It is your responsibility and right to say yes or no regarding eating, drinking, and work. It is your right to say yes or no regarding sex and other issues relating to your personal boundaries. You have the right to say no to physical or emotional abuse, to make the choices about your own body, and who you want to talk to or be with. You get to plan your time and determine your availability based on your own terms, as long as it does not harm or infringe on the rights of others.

...to have wishes, dreams, and needs, and to fail and learn from your mistakes.

(If you require yourself to be perfect and act perfect, and you regard yourself with a very critical eye and find yourself very critical and regretful if others commit one small mistake, this one is important for you.) It is normal to make mistakes. If something bad happens that you did not intend, then, of course, you should repair the damage, admit the mistake and apologize to anyone it may have affected adversely. It is impossible to be perfect and flawless, but it is possible to be responsible and do the right thing when something does not go according to plan.

Once you consciously begin to live in accordance with your rights, you will get respect and responsiveness from others, and people will take your contribution seriously. A thorough grounding in your own rights will foster the courage to handle what life sends your way.

EXERCISE: WHAT ARE MY RIGHTS?

Notice your choices and behavior in a range of situations over the course of the day, whether at work or with friends, or with family. Ask yourself:

How do I talk about what I am doing?

What kinds of places do I go?

Do I take chances, or do I conspicuously avoid them?

Do I assert my rights in some way in the course of my normal life? How? What about my behavior suggests that I am comfortable and confident in my rights?

Referring back to the list of rights, which ones am I not *laying claim to?*

Am I surprised to be told I have any of the rights on the list? If so, which ones?

Are there some rights I have difficulty embracing? Which ones?

Are there any rights that, deep down inside, I feel don't apply to me? If so, which ones? What situations and circumstances in my life may have instilled that feeling in me?

Do I sense any danger in starting to live and act according to my rights? What do I fear will happen? What, on the other hand, might I gain?

Is there someone in your social circle that you think of as having high self-esteem, someone who is basically confident and self-aware? If so, look to that person as a role model in learning to claim your rights. Regularly remind yourself of your rights by, for example, posting a copy of this chapter's list of rights somewhere where you will see it often.

EXERCISE: WRITE YOUR LIFE STORY

Tell Your Story to Someone You Trust

This final phase of the exercise is not a must, but it can mean a great deal for you.

Now that you have completed your life story (or at least the first draft of it) find one or more people to tell it to. If you have a partner or a best friend, ask to tell it to them. If you are part of a therapy group doing the exercises, you might all take turns telling your life story to the group. It is important that your listener be someone who knows you and you feel comfortable with, someone with the capacity to be present for you and engaged in what you are saying. This is not an audition or a test: It should be a good experience for you.

You deserve to have a witness to what you have been through—that will make you stronger.

14

CHOOSE YOUR VALUES

Values are principles to live by, and the idea of values implies a sense of ethics and morality. Spiritual and civic values, for example, provide a way of living and a method of dealing with other people in ways that benefit a community and strengthen the future. These can include honesty, responsibility, attention, and love. There are also pragmatic values, such as common sense.

These values are aspects of our ability to reflect and have empathy. These functions belong to the neocortex, the part of the human brain that separates us from animals and makes it possible for us to be self-aware and analytical. The problem is, if you are someone who lives with a lot of fear and a sense of being under threat, you will have difficulty taking advantage of this specialized human inheritance. Instead, much of the processing of what goes on around you will shift to your "reptilian brain," where it works in something more like survival mode. Rather than being able to act in a way that reflects your values and the available facts, you see a world reduced to black-and-white, where the prime objective is self-preservation.

Raised in a Bottle

The reptilian brain is typically firing on all cylinders in families governed by alcohol. Rules relating to various life situations may not exist, where there seem to be no guiding values for interacting with the world. Once a family member reaches the age when he can leave home and live independently, he finds himself thrust out into the world without a firm set of norms to live by and without the security that comes from knowing right from wrong.

Values guide your way of being in the world with regard to other people and yourself. Conscience is linked to values, which means that when you adhere to your principles, it works to everybody's advantage while failing to live up to them, degrades yourself and others.

Relationships become toxic when values disappear, and a kind of lowest common denominator takes over your interactions with others. Honesty, patience, respect, care, justice, and love can disappear—all those values that may never get spelled out overtly in healthy and strong family relationships but are certainly lived by.

By focusing on values, you can rise above the basest levels of human behavior and begin to live according to a plan that is fundamentally healing. Once we realize which values we want to live by and implement them, our self-esteem benefits. Our relationships with other people can grow strong and stable, rather than being mired in the sort of conflict that is more characteristic of our reptilian brain.

Living with values means being able to build a future with other people. It strengthens your independence and strength as a human being, on the one hand, while enriching your relationships with other people on the other, enhancing your ability to be part of something bigger than yourself. A strong set of values nurtures both.

Living in Integrity

On the most fundamental level, living up to your own values requires honesty, and sometimes that can be hard to come by in families where an addiction rules the roost. The amount of lying and denial can be substantial, and getting to the truth is difficult. Not all values are life-affirming, and there may be some not-so-positive values you may have adapted to survive and thrive in that environment. It is important that you track these down and unmask them.

Are there things that you are in denial about? Are there areas of your life where you devalue honesty or where you think trustworthiness doesn't matter? Consider the degree of honesty you engaged in while growing up—was it normal to lie in some situations? Is it still? What level of honesty do you maintain in your most intimate relationships? When strong feelings arise, do you avoid revealing them because you worry about the other person's reaction? Does that course of action, in turn, set off a chain of other lies?

Living up to your values requires you to understand other people's points of view and listen to them, but also to look at yourself objectively. What kind of tone of voice am I using? What kind of expression do I have on my face? What impression is my behavior making? What prompted me to act in the way I'm acting? Did my action come from a pure heart, or am I instead engaged in some kind of power play?

Be honest with yourself. You will make mistakes in your effort to be the best version of yourself, but just keep putting one foot in front of the other. And if something you do causes damage, do your best to make amends and repair the situation.

A healthy set of values and principles can be a complete set of tools for coping with life's challenges. Consciously pursuing them will give you strength and resilience to take on challenges you previously may have tried to avoid.

EXERCISE: YOUR FIVE MOST IMPORTANT VALUES

All these principles/values give inner strength when transformed into action.

From the list below, select five values that, ideally, would form the centerpiece of your life and your relationships.

Tolerance, Acknowledgment, Attention, Respect,

Honesty, Authenticity, Transparency, Willingness,

Surrender, Humility, Forgiveness, Gratitude,

Reason, Hope, Faith, Wisdom, Courage, Strength, Dignity,

Perseverance, Discipline, Skill, Responsibility, Free Will,

Cohesion, Community, Equality, Justice, Empathy,

Compassion, Kindness, Respect, Confidence, Commitment,

Reliability, Patience, Attentiveness, Acceptance, Helpfulness,

Caring, Love, Integrity, Thoroughness, Precision,

Tolerance, Accessibility, Flexibility, Spaciousness, Peace,

Predictability, Loyalty, Engagement

Are there any values of your own that are not listed here? Add them to the list.

Which values did you grow up with in your family?

Are there values you grew up with that you have since lost touch with?

Of the five that you selected above, how might other people see them reflected in your life now?

Do you ever find yourself compromising your values? How does that work out?

What will and can you do in the future to embody your values?

Facing challenges presents very concrete opportunities to live by your values. If you find yourself faced with a challenge of some sort, try interpreting and handling it in terms of three of the values you selected. See if viewing the situation through the lens of those values provides a new way of looking at it and perhaps an unexpected strategy for dealing with it. Imagine other people seeing evidence of your values in the course you take.

(This exercise is based on the author's training in therapist Craig Nakken's approach to working with families shaped by alcohol.)

15

BELIEVE IN THE FUTURE

The effort you have made so far in reading this book and doing the exercises will help you confront and reject the idea that you are somehow cursed and can't share in the same bright future as other people. Not daring to believe in tomorrow is a relic of an upbringing in which the future was either ignored or never allowed to turn out as promised.

It was your parents' job to teach you social skills and help you on your way to being integrated into society. But maybe, like so many parents in alcoholic households, they failed in those responsibilities and left you uncertain about how to relate to the rest of the world. You may never have learned to imagine yourself being good at something or to have high expectations of life.

But that was then. Now you must become a warrior on behalf of your own life, no longer a victim or prisoner of things that happened when you were growing up. You cannot change your childhood, but you can undo its damage, strengthen your self-esteem, peace of mind, and relationship with your body. You can be, and are, the equal of peers whose upbringings were easier than your own.

If you still cling to the idea that such improvements are too good to be true, recognize that as a mechanism meant to protect you from the pain of your childhood, having low expectations was a strategy to shield yourself from disappointment. But that strategy is now obsolete. The fact that you picked up this book indicates that you are already in a different and better place.

Be a Warrior Instead of a Victim in Your Own Life

Do you take responsibility for your own life, or do you let others dictate the outcome? If it's the latter, it is time to make a change. You are an adult, and you have that power. One insight that this book has offered is that it is ultimately yourself who must choose to be a warrior instead of a victim.

The victim follows a path that other people dictate. Other people's lives take priority over her own, and the result is that she ends up living a kind of shadow life, in which her own sense of powerlessness becomes an excuse for not living life to the fullest. The temptation to take on the victim's role is that looking to other people for your guidance and identity actually renders you unaccountable to anyone—you can always claim that it's not your fault that the world is in the state it's in.

Choosing instead to become a warrior, you will experience a sense of power that comes with claiming your own life and your freedom. Where a victim takes no risks for fear of being hurt or disappointed, a warrior takes responsibility and has faith in his resources. Make your choice. Say to yourself, "*This* is how I want to live my life. *These* are the values I want to live by. *This* is what makes sense to me."

Is living by your own principles entirely free of risk? No. There is always a risk that someone will not be able to accept what you are doing for yourself, and they will reject you. But what you receive in return is the chance to feel alive and true to yourself. There is a qualitative difference between these two ways of living in the world.

There are some things that, even as a warrior, you will not be able to do anything about. For example, your parent won't simply stop drinking because you have changed your outlook. But you can decide how you want to cope with these things. As a warrior, you always have the last word: *This is how I choose to handle it.*

Many great personalities can be inspiring models—Nelson Mandela, Desmond Tutu, Rosa Parks, Gandhi, Martin Luther King, Ingrid Betancourt, Mother Teresa—people who have in some instances been kept in captivity but who never stopped being warriors in their own lives and living by their values…and in fact, got the last word after all.

Being an adult is about surveying the entire range of your experiences and taking what you want and need. Not everything about your upbringing deserves to be discarded. There may well be legacies from your father and mother that you care about, which can enrich your life. Some of these, you may even be reluctant to acknowledge. But it's all there for you to pick and choose from, to shape a life that makes sense for you. Adult life is about finding the norms and values you want to live by and embracing them.

Put Stars on the Horizon

The sense of a future disappears in homes under the influence of an addiction—the alcoholic is so trapped in her addiction that she can't look beyond the present needy moment. Plans are always subject to cancelation and disruption, so the future never gets a chance to ripen. Nothing can be relied upon.

But a big part of healing yourself involves making plans, having things to look forward to, and invest in. Call it, "putting stars on the horizon." What would I like to do next year? What will we do this summer as a family? Being happy is important, and *planning* to be happy is important, especially for families with children, for whom everyday life can be awash in duties. Dreaming and planning are essential.

You may have been disappointed so many times that to avoid it happening again, you stopped believing in the possibility of having fun. This is a typical response on the part of someone who grew up in a family shaped by an addiction, a way of coping with the unpredictability and degradation of alcoholism. Now you must see through that defense mechanism and start making plans. You may still not fully believe that the future can be good for you, but you have to cultivate plans and dreams anyway.

Step over your old, broken dreams, the remnants of pain and hopelessness from your past, and move on. Have faith. Make plans for the future, even if you realize that they may meet resistance—after all, you've been caught up for a long time in worries, anxieties, and isolation. You must stop feeding into those negative thoughts. Start working consciously toward your goals and wishes for the future and begin to visualize them. The more you practice this, the more achievable those goals and wishes will seem.

Developing a willingness to feed into hope and positivity is part of the process of learning to take care of yourself. It is uplifting to choose to do something good for yourself, and daring to take on life's challenges, even without guarantees as to how they'll turn out, is an abundant source of energy.

Open your eyes. There may have been so much darkness and dysfunction in your life that you came to believe that to be worried, sad, and always serious is to be "realistic." But that is not true: You are the one who determines whether the glass is half empty or half full.

Picture yourself as someone who feels good, as someone who is allowed to be happy. Don't look to your parents to model your moods for you. They have their feelings, and you have yours, and you do not help anyone by worrying about it. Likewise, it does not hurt your mother that you walk around happy even though she is still drinking. To dream well is to live well, and you are allowed to dream well.

EXERCISES: GOALS AND WISHES

Many children and young people in families with alcohol problems have experienced looking forward to something that ultimately got derailed by their parents' problems. If you have not begun to work with the wounds and disappointments that are often associated with an upbringing in a family shaped by alcohol, you may butt up against ingrained habits developed as defenses against failure or disappointment. Your attention may habitually be focused on things that can go wrong rather than things that can go well or are, in fact, going well already. But you must take the plunge. Dare to set goals. Dare to wish and dare to be happy.

1. What Makes You Happy?

Name five activities that make you happy. Enumerating them will guide you in choosing activities that create joy. How do you currently practice these activities?

. . .

2. Goals

Name some goals you will try to achieve in the next two months. Name only those you know you will be able to achieve. What will it mean to you to fulfill any of those goals?

3. Recognize Positive Situations

At the end of the day, make a list of your good experiences, from waking up in the morning until you go to bed. Assign scores to them: "I slept well last night—1 point." "My partner is sitting here beside me—2 points." And so on.

Inventory all the things you can think of that went well and that you are grateful for. You may find that you take some of these for granted and don't enjoy them as much as you should. Try to refresh your images of those things and give them back their meaning.

Write a letter to yourself that includes:

• Recognition of your work with yourself through this book and in other contexts.

• Recognition of yourself as a child and a teenager, and all the things you did.

• Recognition of yourself as an adult and all that you are doing now.

• A description of where you would like your work with yourself to have brought you six months from now.

• Some wishes for yourself—the stars on your horizon.

Choose realistic wishes that really matter to you and whose fulfillment will make you happy or improve your situation. Don't hide them: Write them down in multiple places, say them out *loud, talk about them with others. Once you have finished this letter to yourself, give it to a friend you can trust and ask him to mail it to you exactly six months from today.*

It is healthier and more beneficial for your psyche to focus on success than failure, on things you want to achieve rather than things you're afraid of or deeply want to avoid. Practice turning your focus to these positive areas daily—take a break from your worries and your fantasies that things that could go wrong.

FINAL THOUGHTS
WHERE DO I GO FROM HERE?

Your great, careful work with this book is important to your healing process. The discomfort you may have experienced, the feelings you've had to face up to, your sometimes uncomfortable recognition of the patterns your family followed, and your role in them—all that has significance, and all of it will bear fruit. The pain that delving into your story may cause you is no longer the result of a failure; it is not some kind of continuation of the bad things you already experienced in life. Instead, it's a realization, a pinpointing of where something wasn't right and good.

There are aspects of yourself that you didn't get the chance to fully develop, roles you had to play that were not the real you. In that respect, you let yourself down for, perhaps, many years. The purpose of this book is to get things into their proper place and tip the balance in the right direction. Be honest: There are relationships that stand in your way and that you will need to get rid of. Your archetypal role, your dependency, your denial, your shame, the nagging voices of your parents in your mind—all those things will need to be cast out, so you can see yourself as who you really are.

This book has heaped a lot on your plate, and you may have found it chaotic to deal with so much at once. But all the parameters and mechanisms you've been exploring and adjusting along the way are now activated. You can now begin to view life as safe, strengthen your self-esteem, and put some trust in your own instincts and actions. You can stand on your own two feet and interact with other people without fear. Yes, the work so far has been complicated and daunting, but it will pay off.

This book was written to help you see just how your parent's substance abuse affected your family and make you aware that you and your troubles are not the same thing. In the face of addiction, nothing is sacred. Alcoholism (or any other addiction) is so powerful that if it is not stopped, it will overwhelm everything—even the most powerful force in the universe, a mother's love for her child.

That's the monster you had to contend with as you grew up, and now you have a clearer idea of how it shaped and dominated your life. Hopefully, your patience for adapting to unpleasant situations at all costs has finally run out, and you will demand more for yourself. You will demand every bit as much as you deserve.

Who am I? Who am I in relation to other people? What can I do? What kind of place is this world? These are essential questions crucial to each human being's development. They concern who we become as individuals and how we connect—or don't—with other people.

Unfortunately, they are precisely the issues that get muddled and skewed in a family influenced by alcohol abuse. The children look to the parents as models of how to be and behave, whether alone or with others, without realizing that the model their parents present is distorted and dysfunctional, not the kind of training that lays the groundwork for a happy, healthy life. This book has tried to give you an objective look at that process and how it has affected you.

Completing the House

Remember that shaky house we talked about back at the beginning? Take another look—you may not recognize it now. The holes in the foundation have been filled in. The walls are sturdy; the ceilings are sound. The rooms shelter and protect their occupants now and draw clear boundaries between life inside and outside. The doors open and close, lock and unlock, so you control who is allowed to enter. Warm and comfortable, this is no longer a construction project but a finished home, fit for making a life in.

Childhood in a family impacted by alcohol abuse can be a sort of prison. You don't get to talk about yourself or draw attention to your own needs; you don't get to ask for explanations of things you do not understand. That prolonged trauma left you with a void inside. But your feelings of loneliness, of isolation, of being an outsider, have persisted long enough.

It is time to discover your real self and discard the illusory, damaged self you are familiar with. All that belongs to the past, and thanks to your work in this book and elsewhere, a change for the better is well underway.

You have done this for your own sake. You have done it because you believe that life has more to offer than the wreckage your parents left behind. You have done it because you understand that you are worth the investment of time and effort and emotion if it means being able to say, "I am no longer going to be alone. I am *not* alone."

And you are right.

Acknowledgments

Heartfelt thanks to Lisa Favero for her multiple roles in our collaboration. I am deeply grateful for her skills as both translator and project manager. Engaged and tireless, she has shown a precise understanding and sense of what I wanted to do with this book.

My thanks also to copyeditor Barry Foy for his keen eye—he found my voice and helped keep it coherent, wherever language and translation work threatened to get in the way and blur the message. And my appreciation to designer Patrick Kelly for making and revising drawings and models.

A big thank-you to Jasmina Nielsen for her monumental help with all the visible and invisible elements of the last phase of the work: research, website, feedback, etc. Working with her has been a huge gift.

Last but not least, a multitude of thanks to my family. You have been nothing but supportive of the effort, always patient with the work it took me to finish this book, night after night, for a couple of years. And for your ongoing enthusiasm over and interest in the process, I express my gratitude to my wise and lovely son, August.

Notes

Chapter 1. Facing the Reality of Families Shaped by Alcohol Problems

1.

Allen, J.G. & Fonagy, P. (eds.) (2006): Handbook of Mentalization-Based Treatment. Chichester: John Wiley & Sons.

https://www.wiley.com/en-us/The+Handbook+of+Mentalization+Based+Treatment-p-9780470015605

Chapter 2. Learning to "Hold Mind in Mind"

1.

Lander, Laura; Howsare, Janie and Byrne, Marilyn: The Impact of Substance Use Disorders on Families and Children: From Theory to Practice

https://www.ncbi.nlm.nih.gov/pmc/articles/PMC3725219/

Haverfield, Marie C. and Theiss, Jennifer A. (2015). Parent's alcoholism severity and family topic avoidance about alcohol as predictors of perceived stigma among adult children of alcoholics: Implications for emotional and psychological resilience. Health Communication. 2016;31(5):606-16

Download citation https://doi.org/10.1080/10410236.2014.981665

https://www.tandfonline.com/doi/abs/10.1080/10410236.2014.981665

Chapter 3. Telling Your Own Story

1.

Fonagy, Peter (2001). Attachment Theory and Psychoanalysis. New York, Other Press.

https://psychoanalysis.org.uk/our-authors-and-theorists/peter-fonagy

Fonagy, Peter and Campbell, Chloe. Attachment Theory and Mentalizing

http://discovery.ucl.ac.uk/1476997/1/Fonagy_Revisions_Attachment%20Theory%20and%20Mentalizing.pdf

Lander, Laura; Howsare, Janie and Byrne, Marilyn. The Impact of Substance Use Disorders on Families and Children: From Theory to Practice

https://www.ncbi.nlm.nih.gov/pmc/articles/PMC3725219/

Bowlby, J. (1988): A Secure Base: Parent-Child Attachment and Healthy Human Development. Tavistock professional book. London: Routledge. ISBN 0-422-62230-3. OCLC 42913724.

Also full-text link here:

https://pdfs.semanticscholar.org/545b/983942722792c0e0c48b699aced98323d13e.pdf

Stern, Daniel N. (1985 and 1998): The Interpersonal World of the Infant: A View from Psychoanalysis and Development. ISBN 978-0-465-03403-1

https://en.wikipedia.org/wiki/The_Interpersonal_World_of_the_Infant

Goleman, Daniel (1986): Child Development Theory Stresses Small Moments; Oct. 21, 1986

https://www.nytimes.com/1986/10/21/science/child-development-theory-stresses-small-moments.html

---

Chapter 5. Emotional Triggers

1.

Seidenfaden, Kirsten, and P. Draiby. *The Vibrant Relationship: A Handbook for Couples and Therapists.* London: Routledge, 2018.

Johnson, Sue. *Hold Me Tight: Seven Conversations for a Lifetime of Love.* Boston: Little, Brown and Company, 2008.

http://drsuejohnson.com/books/hold-me-tight/

Chapter 6. Self-Esteem

1.

Robins, Richard W. and Trzesniewski, Kali H. (2005). Self-Esteem Development Across the Lifespan.

https://doi.org/10.1111/j.0963-7214.2005.00353.x

https://journals.sagepub.com/doi/abs/10.1111/j.0963-7214.2005.00353.x

From https://en.wikipedia.org/wiki/Self-esteem

Raboteg-Saric Z.; Sakic M. (2014). "Relations of parenting styles and friendship quality to self-esteem, life satisfaction, & happiness in adolescents". Applied Research in the Quality of Life. 9 (3): 749–765. DOI:10.1007/s11482-013-9268-0.

Olsen, J. M.; Breckler, S. J.; Wiggins, E. C. (2008). Social Psychology Alive (First Canadian ed.). Toronto: Thomson Nelson. ISBN 978-0-17-622452-3.

Coopersmith, S. (1967). The Antecedents of Self-Esteem. New York: W. H. Freeman.

Isberg, R. S.; Hauser, S. T.; Jacobson, A. M.; Powers, S. I.; Noam, G.; Weiss-Perry, B.; Fullansbee, D. (1989). "Parental contexts of adolescent self-esteem: A developmental perspective". Journal of Youth and Adolescence. 18 (1): 1–23. DOI:10.1007/BF02139243. PMID 24271601.

Lamborn, S. D.; Mounts, N. S.; Steinberg, L.; Dornbusch, S. M. (1991). "Patterns of Competence and Adjustment among Adolescents from Authoritative, Authoritarian, Indulgent, and Neglectful Families". Child Development. 62(5): 1049–1065. DOI:10.1111/j.1467-8624.1991.tb01588.x. PMID 1756655.

"Self-Esteem." Self-Esteem. N.p., n.d. Web. 27 Nov. 2012.

https://cmhc.utexas.edu/selfesteem.html

2.

Rangarajan, Sripriya (2008). Mediators and Moderators of Parental Alcoholism Effects on Offspring Self-Esteem; Alcohol and Alcoholism, Volume 43, Issue 4, July-August 2008, Pages 481–491, https://doi.org/10.1093/alcalc/agn034

https://academic.oup.com/alcalc/article/43/4/481/128794

Oshri, Assaf; Carlson, Matthew W.; Kwon, Josephine A.; Zeichner, Amos; Wickrama, K. A. S. Kandauda (2017). Developmental Growth Trajectories of Self-Esteem in Adolescence: Associations with Child Neglect and Drug Use and Abuse in Young Adulthood. Journal of Youth and Adolescence

January 2017, Volume 46, Issue 1, pp 151–164.

https://link.springer.com/article/10.1007/s10964-016-0483-5

Park, Sihyun; Schepp, Karen G.(2015). A Systematic Review of Research on Children of Alcoholics: Their Inherent Resilience and Vulnerability. Journal of Child and Family Studies May 2015, Volume 24, Issue 5, pp 1222–1231

https://link.springer.com/article/10.1007/s10826-014-9930-7

3.

https://mct-institute.co.uk/

Wells, Adrian (2009). Metacognitive Therapy for Anxiety and Depression. Guilford Publications.

https://www.guilford.com/excerpts/wells.pdf?t

Fisher, Peter L.; Wells, Adrian (2009). Metacognitive therapy: distinctive features. The CBT distinctive features series. London;

New York: Routledge. ISBN 9780415434980. OCLC 229466109.

Normann, Nicoline and Morina, Nexhmedin (2018). The Efficacy of Metacognitive Therapy: A Systematic Review and Meta-Analysis. Frontiers in Psychology. 2018; 9: 2211. DOI: 10.3389/fpsyg.2018.02211

PMCID: PMC6246690

PMID: 30487770

https://www.ncbi.nlm.nih.gov/pmc/articles/PMC6246690/

Chapter 7. Letting Go of Trauma and Grounding Yourself in Your Body

1.

Belliveau J.M.; Stoppard J. M. (1995). Parental alcohol abuse and gender as predictors of psychopathology in adult children of alcoholics. Addictive Behaviors. 1995 Sep-Oct;20(5):619-25.

https://www.ncbi.nlm.nih.gov/pubmed/8712059

WHO. Child maltreatment and alcohol (2006).

https://www.who.int/violence_injury_prevention/violence/world_report/factsheets/fs_child.pdf

Christoffersen M. N.; Soothill, K. (2003). The long-term consequences of parental alcohol abuse: a cohort study of children in Denmark. Journal of Substance Abuse Treatment. 2003 Sep;25(2):107-16.

https://www.ncbi.nlm.nih.gov/pubmed/14629993

Jacob, T.; Windle, M.; Seilhamer, R. A.; and Bost, J. (1999). Adult children of alcoholics: Drinking, psychiatric, and psychosocial status. Psychology of Addictive Behaviors, 13(1), 3-21.

http://dx.doi.org/10.1037/0893-164X.13.1.3

https://psycnet.apa.org/record/1999-10038-001

Klostermann, Keith and Kelley, Michelle L. (2009). Alcoholism and Intimate Partner Violence: Effects on Children's Psychosocial Adjustment. International Journal of Environmental Research and Public Health. 2009 Dec; 6(12): 3156–3168. DOI: 10.3390/ijerph6123156

PMCID: PMC2800341

PMID: 20049253

https://www.ncbi.nlm.nih.gov/pmc/articles/PMC2800341/

Jayne, Mark and Valentine, Gill (2016). Childhood, Family, Alcohol. London: Imprint Routledge.

DOI https://doi.org/10.4324/9781315260549

eBook ISBN 9781315260549

https://www.taylorfrancis.com/books/9781315260549

Potter-Efron, Ron and Potter-Efron, Patricia (1990). Aggression, Family Violence and Chemical Dependency. New York: Imprint Routledge.

DOI https://doi.org/10.4324/9781315784588

eBook ISBN 9781315784588

https://www.taylorfrancis.com/books/9781315784588

2.

Somatic Experiencing – Continuing Education

https://traumahealing.org/about-us/

Levine, Peter A. *Waking the Tiger: Healing Trauma.* Berkeley, CA: North Atlantic Books, 1997.

Levine, Peter A. (Author) and van der Kolk, Bessel A. (Foreword) (2015). Trauma and Memory: Brain and Body in a Search for the Living Past: A Practical Guide for Understanding and Working with Traumatic Memory. North Atlantic Books. ISBN-10: 1583949941

Chapter 8. Needs—Met and Unmet

1.

http://www.ericberne.com/

Berne, Eric (1996). Games People Play: The Basic Handbook of Transactional Analysis. Ballantine Books. ISBN-10: 9780345410030

Berne, Eric (2015). Transactional Analysis in Psychotherapy: A Systematic Individual and Social Psychiatry. Martino Fine Books. ISBN-10: 161427844X

2.

Hinrichs, J.; DeFife, J.; Westen, D. (2011). Personality subtypes in adolescent and adult children of alcoholics: A two-part study.

"Children of alcoholics (COAs) are at three to four times the risk for developing alcoholism than a child without an alcoholic parent, and daughters of alcoholics are more likely to marry alcoholic men, perpetuating the cycle to future generations (Obot et al., 2001)." The Journal of Nervous and Mental Disease. 2011 Jul; 199(7): 487–498. DOI: 10.1097/NMD.0b013e3182214268

PMCID: PMC3143015

NIHMSID: NIHMS300039

PMID: 21716063

https://www.ncbi.nlm.nih.gov/pmc/articles/PMC3143015/

Obot, I.S.; Wagner, F.A.; Anthony, J.C. (2001). Early onset and recent drug use among children of parents with alcohol problems: data from a national epidemiologic survey. Drug and Alcohol Dependence. 2001 Dec 1;65(1):1-8.

https://www.ncbi.nlm.nih.gov/pubmed/11714584

Solis, Jessica M.; Shadur, Julia M.; Burns, Alison R. and Hussong, Andrea M. (2012). Understanding the Diverse Needs of Children whose Parents Abuse Substances. Current Drug Abuse Reviews. 2012 Jun; 5(2): 135–147.

PMCID: PMC3676900

NIHMSID: NIHMS473560

PMID: 22455509

https://www.ncbi.nlm.nih.gov/pmc/articles/PMC3676900/

Dube, Shanta R.; Anda, Robert F.; Felitti, Vincent J.; Edwards, Valerie J.; Croft, Janet B. (2002). Adverse childhood experiences and personal alcohol abuse as an adult. Addictive Behaviors Volume 27, Issue 5, September–October 2002, Pages 713-725

https://doi.org/10.1016/S0306-4603(01)00204-0

https://www.sciencedirect.com/science/article/abs/pii/S0306460301002040

Jennison, K.M.; Johnson, K. A. (1998). Alcohol dependence in adult children of alcoholics: longitudinal evidence of early risk. Journal of Drug Education 1998;28(1):19-37.

https://www.ncbi.nlm.nih.gov/pubmed/9567578

Bibliography

BOOKS

Allen, Jon G., and Peter Fonagy (eds.). *Handbook of Mentalization-Based Treatment*. Chichester, UK: John Wiley & Sons, 2006.

Allen, Jon G., P. Fonagy, and A.W. Bateman. *Mentalizing in Clinical Practice*. Washington, DC: American Psychiatric Publishing, 2008.

Bechsgaard, Camilla Carlsen, and Katrine Krebs. *FamilieFred med dine forældre* [Finding harmony with your parents]. Copenhagen: Dansk Psykologisk Forlag, 2012.

Berne, Eric. *Games People Play: The Basic Handbook of Transactional Analysis*. New York: Ballantine Books, 1996.

Berne, Eric. *Transactional Analysis in Psychotherapy: A Systematic Individual and Social Psychiatry*. Eastford, CT: Martino Fine Books, 2015.

Bowlby, John. *The Making and Breaking of Affectional Bonds*. London: Routledge, 2005.

Bowlby, John. *A Secure Base: Parent-Child Attachment and Healthy Human Development*. London: Routledge, 1988.

Breckler, Steven J., James Olson, and Elizabeth Wiggins. *Social Psychology Alive*. Belmont, CA: Wadsworth Publishing Company, 2005.

Christensen, Else. "Børn i familier med alkohol og stofproblemer" [Children in families with alcohol and drug problems]. *Forebyggelse og hygiejne 18*. Copenhagen: Sundhedsstyrelsen, 1992.

Coopersmith, Stanley. *The Antecedents of Self-Esteem*. New York: W.H. Freeman & Company, 1967.

Fisher, Peter, and Adrian Wells. *Metacognitive Therapy* (The CBT Distinctive Features Series). London: Routledge, 2009.

Fonagy, Peter. *Attachment Theory and Psychoanalysis*. New York: Other Press, 2001.

Gerhardt, Sue. *Kærlighed gør en forskel. Kærlige følelser former barnets hjerne* [Love makes a difference: Feelings of love shape a child's brain]. Copenhagen: Dansk Psykologisk Forlag, 2004.

Gullestrup, Lise. *At blive et med sig selv – om udviklingen af det 0-5 årige barns selv* [Becoming one with the self: On the development of the 0- to 5-year-old child's identity]. Copenhagen: Frydenlund, 2009.

Hanson, Torben. *Assertions Træning, selvtillid, sikkerhed, gennemslagskraft* [Assertion training, confidence, security, agency]. Copenhagen: Borgen, 1996.

Hart, Susan, and Rikke Schwartz. *Fra interaktion til relation* [From interacting to relating]. Copenhagen: Hans Reitzels Forlag, 2008.

Hay, Louise L. *I Can Do It: How to Use Affirmations to Change Your Life*. Carlsbad, CA: Hay House, 2003.

Hay, Louise L. *You Can Heal Your Life*. Carlsbad, CA: Hay House, 1984.

Heller, Laurence, and Aline LaPierre. *Healing Developmental Trauma: How Early Trauma Affects Self-Regulation, Self-Image, and the Capacity for Relationship*. Berkeley, CA: North Atlantic Books, 2012.

Hendrix, Harville. *Getting the Love You Want*. New York: Owl/Holt, 1988.

Hertz, Berit, et al. *Anerkendelse i børnehøjde* [Recognition from a child's point of view]. Copenhagen: Dansk Psykologisk Forlag, 2006.

Jayne, Mark, and Gill Valentine. *Childhood, Family, Alcohol*. London: Routledge, 2016.

Johnson, Sue. *Hold Me Tight: Seven Conversations for a Lifetime of Love*. Boston: Little, Brown and Company, 2008.

Josefsson, Dan, and Egil Linge. *Kærligheden. Fra første øjekast til et varigt forhold* [Love at first sight to a lasting relationship]. Copenhagen: Borgen, 2014.

Levine, Peter A. *Healing Trauma: A Pioneering Program for Restoring the Wisdom of Your Body*. Louisville, CO: Sounds True, 2008.

Levine, Peter A. *In an Unspoken Voice: How the Body Releases Trauma and Restores Goodness*. Berkeley, CA: North Atlantic Books, 2010.

Levine, Peter A. (author) and Bessel A. van der Kolk (foreword). *Trauma and Memory: Brain and Body in a Search for the Living*

Past: *A Practical Guide for Understanding and Working with Traumatic Memory*. Berkeley, CA: North Atlantic Books, 2015.

Levine, Peter A. *Waking the Tiger: Healing Trauma*. Berkeley, CA: North Atlantic Books, 1997.

Lindgaard, Helle. *Voksne børn fra familier med alkoholproblemer – mestring og modstandsdygtighed* [Adult children from families with alcohol problems: Coping and resilience]. Århus: Center for rusmiddelforskning, Aarhus universitet, 2004.

Mackrill, Thomas. *Håndbog til unge og voksne fra familier med alkoholproblemer* [Manual for young adults and adults from families with alcohol problems]. Copenhagen: Dansk Psykologisk Forlag, 2011.

Nakken, Craig. *The Addictive Personality: Understanding the Addictive Process and Compulsive Behavior.* Center City, MN: Hazelden, 2009.

Oestrich, Irene Henriette. *Selvværd og nye færdigheder – manual til dig i udvikling* [Self-worth and new capabilities: A handbook for your development]. Viborg: Dansk Psykologisk Forlag, 2010.

Potter-Efron, Ron, and Patricia Potter-Efron. *Aggression, Family Violence and Chemical Dependency*. London: Routledge, 1990.

Schore, Allan N. "Parent-Infant Communication and the Neurobiology of Emotional Development." Paper presented at the Head Start National Research Conference, Washington, DC, June 28–July 1, 2000.

Seidenfaden, Kirsten, and Piet Draiby. *The Vibrant Family: A Handbook for Parents and Professionals*. London: Routledge, 2011.

Seidenfaden, Kirsten, and Piet Draiby. *The Vibrant Relationship: A Handbook for Couples and Therapists.* London: Routledge, 2018.

Smith, Lars. *Tilknytning og børns udvikling* [Attachment and child development]. Copenhagen: Akademisk Forlag, 2003.

Stern, Daniel N. *The Interpersonal World of the Infant: A View from Psychoanalysis and Developmental Psychology.* New York: Basic Books, 2000.

Thormann, Inger, and Charlotte Guldberg. *Hånden på hjertet. Omsorg for det lille barn i krise* [Hand to heart: Compassion for the small child in crisis]. Copenhagen: Hans Reitzels Forlag, 2004.

Trembacz, Birgit. *Familier med alkoholmonstre. Forståelse, respekt, forandring* [Families haunted by alcoholism: Understanding, respect, and transformation]. Viborg: Dansk Psykologisk Forlag, 2011.

Trembacz, Birgit. *Vokset op med alkoholproblemer. Barndom og voksenliv – konsekvenser, modstandskraft og frigørelse* [Raised with alcohol problems: Childhood and adult life— consequences, resilience, and freedom]. Viborg: Dansk Psykologisk Forlag, 2009.

Wallroth, Per. *Mentaliseringsbogen* [The mentalizing book]. Copenhagen: Hans Reitzels Forlag, 2014.

Wells, Adrian. *Metacognitive Therapy for Anxiety and Depression.* New York: Guilford Press, 2009.

Wennerberg, Tor. *Vi er vores relationer. Om tilknytning, traumer og dissociation* [We are our relationships: On bonding, trauma, and dissociation]. Viborg: Dansk Psykologisk Forlag, 2014.

JOURNAL AND PERIODICAL ARTICLES

Belliveau J.M.; Stoppard J. M. (1995). Parental alcohol abuse and gender as predictors of psychopathology in adult children of alcoholics. Addictive Behaviors. 1995 Sep-Oct;20(5):619-25.

https://www.ncbi.nlm.nih.gov/pubmed/8712059

Christoffersen M. N.; Soothill, K. (2003). The long-term consequences of parental alcohol abuse: a cohort study of children in Denmark. Journal of Substance Abuse Treatment. 2003 Sep;25(2):107-16.

https://www.ncbi.nlm.nih.gov/pubmed/14629993

Dube, Shanta R.; Anda, Robert F.; Felitti, Vincent J.; Edwards, Valerie J.; Croft, Janet B. (2002). Adverse childhood experiences and personal alcohol abuse as an adult. Addictive Behaviors Volume 27, Issue 5, September–October 2002, Pages 713-725

https://doi.org/10.1016/S0306-4603(01)00204-0

https://www.sciencedirect.com/science/article/abs/pii/S0306460301002040

Goleman, Daniel (1986): Child Development Theory Stresses Small Moments; Oct. 21, 1986

https://www.nytimes.com/1986/10/21/science/child-development-theory-stresses-small-moments.html

Haverfield, Marie C. and Theiss, Jennifer A. (2015). Parent's alcoholism severity and family topic avoidance about alcohol as predictors of perceived stigma among adult children of alcoholics: Implications for emotional and psychological resilience. Health Communication. 2016;31(5):606-16

Download citation https://doi.org/10.1080/10410236.2014.981665

https://www.tandfonline.com/doi/abs/10.1080/10410236.2014.981665

Hinrichs, J.; DeFife, J.; Westen, D. (2011). Personality subtypes in adolescent and adult children of alcoholics: A two part study.

"Children of alcoholics (COAs) are at three to four times the risk for developing alcoholism than a child without an alcoholic parent, and daughters of alcoholics are more likely to marry alcoholic men, perpetuating the cycle to future generations (Obot et al., 2001)." The Journal of Nervous and Mental Disease. 2011 Jul; 199(7): 487–498. DOI: 10.1097/NMD.0b013e3182214268

PMCID: PMC3143015

NIHMSID: NIHMS300039

PMID: 21716063

https://www.ncbi.nlm.nih.gov/pmc/articles/PMC3143015/

Isberg, R. S.; Hauser, S. T.; Jacobson, A. M.; Powers, S. I.; Noam, G.; Weiss-Perry, B.; Fullansbee, D. (1989). "Parental contexts of adolescent self-esteem: A developmental perspective". Journal of Youth and Adolescence. 18 (1): 1–23. DOI:10.1007/BF02139243. PMID 24271601.

Jacob, T.; Windle, M.; Seilhamer, R. A.; and Bost, J. (1999). Adult children of alcoholics: Drinking, psychiatric, and psychosocial status. Psychology of Addictive Behaviors, 13(1), 3-21.

http://dx.doi.org/10.1037/0893-164X.13.1.3

https://psycnet.apa.org/record/1999-10038-001

Jennison, K.M.; Johnson, K. A. (1998). Alcohol dependence in adult children of alcoholics: longitudinal evidence of early risk. Journal of Drug Education 1998;28(1):19-37.

https://www.ncbi.nlm.nih.gov/pubmed/9567578

Klostermann, Keith and Kelley, Michelle L. (2009). Alcoholism and Intimate Partner Violence: Effects on Children's Psychosocial Adjustment. International Journal of Environmental Research and Public Health. 2009 Dec; 6(12): 3156–3168. DOI: 10.3390/ijerph6123156

PMCID: PMC2800341

PMID: 20049253

https://www.ncbi.nlm.nih.gov/pmc/articles/PMC2800341/

Lamborn, S. D.; Mounts, N. S.; Steinberg, L.; Dornbusch, S. M. (1991). "Patterns of Competence and Adjustment among Adolescents from Authoritative, Authoritarian, Indulgent, and Neglectful Families". Child Development. 62(5): 1049–1065. DOI:10.1111/j.1467-8624.1991.tb01588.x. PMID 1756655.

Normann, Nicoline and Morina, Nexhmedin (2018). The Efficacy of Metacognitive Therapy: A Systematic Review and Meta-Analysis. Frontiers in Psychology. 2018; 9: 2211. DOI: 10.3389/fpsyg.2018.02211

PMCID: PMC6246690

PMID: 30487770

https://www.ncbi.nlm.nih.gov/pmc/articles/PMC6246690/

Obot, I.S.; Wagner, F.A.; Anthony, J.C. (2001). Early onset and recent drug use among children of parents with alcohol problems: data from a national epidemiologic survey. Drug and Alcohol Dependence. 2001 Dec 1;65(1):1-8.

https://www.ncbi.nlm.nih.gov/pubmed/11714584

Oshri, Assaf; Carlson, Matthew W.; Kwon, Josephine A.; Zeichner, Amos; Wickrama, K. A. S. Kandauda (2017). Developmental Growth Trajectories of Self-Esteem in Adolescence: Associations with Child Neglect and Drug Use and Abuse in Young Adulthood. Journal of Youth and Adolescence

January 2017, Volume 46, Issue 1, pp 151–164.

https://link.springer.com/article/10.1007/s10964-016-0483-5

Park, Sihyun; Schepp, Karen G.(2015). A Systematic Review of Research on Children of Alcoholics: Their Inherent Resilience and Vulnerability. Journal of Child and Family Studies May 2015, Volume 24, Issue 5, pp 1222–1231

https://link.springer.com/article/10.1007/s10826-014-9930-7

From https://en.wikipedia.org/wiki/Self-esteem

Raboteg-Saric Z.; Sakic M. (2014). "Relations of parenting styles and friendship quality to self-esteem, life satisfaction, & happiness in adolescents". Applied Research in the Quality of Life. 9 (3): 749–765. DOI:10.1007/s11482-013-9268-0

Rangarajan, Sripriya (2008). Mediators and Moderators of Parental Alcoholism Effects on Offspring Self-Esteem; Alcohol and Alcoholism, Volume 43, Issue 4, July-August 2008, Pages 481–491, https://doi.org/10.1093/alcalc/agn034

https://academic.oup.com/alcalc/article/43/4/481/128794

Robins, Richard W. and Trzesniewski, Kali H. (2005). Self-Esteem Development Across the Lifespan.

https://doi.org/10.1111/j.0963-7214.2005.00353.x

https://journals.sagepub.com/doi/abs/10.1111/j.0963-7214.2005.00353.x

Solis, Jessica M.; Shadur, Julia M.; Burns, Alison R. and Hussong, Andrea M. (2012). Understanding the Diverse Needs of Children whose Parents Abuse Substances. Current Drug Abuse Reviews. 2012 Jun; 5(2): 135–147.

PMCID: PMC3676900

NIHMSID: NIHMS473560

PMID: 22455509

https://www.ncbi.nlm.nih.gov/pmc/articles/PMC3676900/

6t576MISCELLANEOUS INTERNET SOURCES

http://www.ericberne.com/

Fonagy, Peter and Campbell, Chloe. Attachment Theory and Mentalizing

http://discovery.ucl.ac.uk/1476997/1/Fonagy_Revisions_Attachment%20Theory%20and%20Mentalizing.pdf

Lander, Laura; Howsare, Janie and Byrne, Marilyn: The Impact of Substance Use Disorders on Families and Children: From Theory to Practice

https://www.ncbi.nlm.nih.gov/pmc/articles/PMC3725219/

https://mct-institute.co.uk/

"Self-Esteem." Self-Esteem. N.p., n.d. Web. 27 Nov. 2012.

https://cmhc.utexas.edu/selfesteem.html

Somatic Experiencing – Continuing Education

https://traumahealing.org/about-us/

Stern, Daniel N. (1985 and 1998): The Interpersonal World of the Infant: A View from Psychoanalysis and Development. ISBN 978-0-465-03403-1 https://en.wikipedia.org/wiki/The_Interpersonal_World_of_the_Infant

WHO. Child maltreatment and alcohol (2006).

https://www.who.int/violence_injury_prevention/violence/world_report/factsheets/fs_child.pdf

About the Author

Kristina Hermann is a psychotherapist and author with a clinic in Copenhagen, Denmark. She has worked with families afflicted by alcohol abuse since 2000, and has written extensively about adult children of alcoholics. In 2015 she published a self-help book in Danish: Du er ikke alene: en opvækst med alkoholproblemer ("You are not alone: An upbringing shaped by alcohol problems"), now in its third printing. **Raised in a Bottle**: A Workbook for Adult Children of Alcoholics (in progress) is her first book in English.

She received her Master degree in Psychology from the University of Aarhus, Denmark in 2012. In addition to her work as a psychotherapist, she also teaches seminars, conducts workshops and is a supervisor of the work of other therapists.

www.ingramcontent.com/pod-product-compliance
Lightning Source LLC
Chambersburg PA
CBHW050859240426
43673CB00033B/495/J